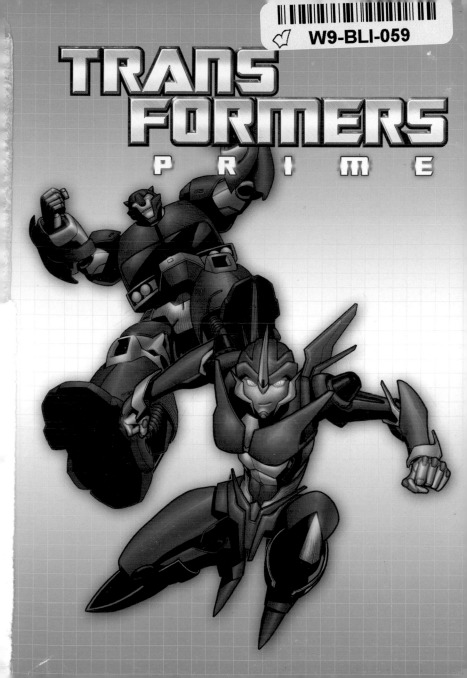

TRANS
FORMERS
P R I M E

Written by **Mike Johnson**

CHAPTER 1
Art by **E.J. Su**
Color by **Andrew Dalhouse**

CHAPTER 2
Pencils by **Atilio Martin** and **Allan Jefferson**
Inks by **Jordi Tarragona, Sergio Abad,** and
Juan An Ramirez
Colors by **Andre Dalhouse**

CHAPTER 3
Pencils by **David Daza**
Inks by **Sergio Abad** and **David Daza**
Colors by **Cam** and **Carlos Aon** for Estudio Haus

CHAPTER 4
Pencils by **Joe St. Pierre**
Inks by **Jonas Trindale**
Colors by **Jorge Blanco** and **Jok** for Estudio Haus

Front and Back Cover Artwork by **Jose Lopez** and **Augusto Barranco**

————————————————————————

Letters by **Chris Mowry** and **Robbie Robbins**
Assistant Edits by **Carlos Guzman**
Edits by **Andy Schmidt**

Special thanks to Hasbro's Aaron Archer, Michael Kelly, Amie Lozanski, Val Roca, Ed Lane, Michael Provost, Erin Hillman, Samantha Lomow, Michael Verrecchia, Jeff Kline, Jose Lopez, Augusta Barranco, and Hasbro Studios for their invaluable assistance

Licensed By:

www.IDWPUBLISHING.com   ISBN: 978-1-60010-832-7   13 12 11 10   1 2 3 4

IDW Publishing is: Operations: Ted Adams, CEO & Publisher • Greg Goldstein, Chief Operating Officer • Matthew Ruzicka, CPA, Chief Financial Officer • Alan Payne, VP of Sales • Lorelei Bunjes, Director of Digital Services • Jeff Webber, Director of ePublishing • AnnaMaria White, Dir. Marketing and Public Relations • Dirk Wood, Dir. Retail Marketing • Marci Hubbard, Executive Assistant • Alonzo Simon, Shipping Manager • Angela Loggins, Staff Accountant • Cherrie Go, Assistant Web Designer • Editorial: Chris Ryall, Chief Creative Officer, Editor-In-Chief • Scott Dunbier, Senior Editor, Special Projects • Andy Schmidt, Senior Editor • Bob Schreck, Senior Editor • Justin Eisinger, Senior Editor, Books • Kris Oprisko, Editor/Foreign Lic. • Denton J. Tipton, Editor • Tom Waltz, Editor • Mariah Huehner, Editor • Carlos Guzman, Assistant Editor • Bobby Curnow, Assistant Editor • Design: Robbie Robbins, EVP/Sr. Graphic Artist • Neil Uyetake, Senior Art Director • Chris Mowry, Senior Graphic Artist • Amauri Osorio, Graphic Artist • Gilberto Lazcano, Production Assistant • Shawn Lee, Graphic Artist

Chapter One

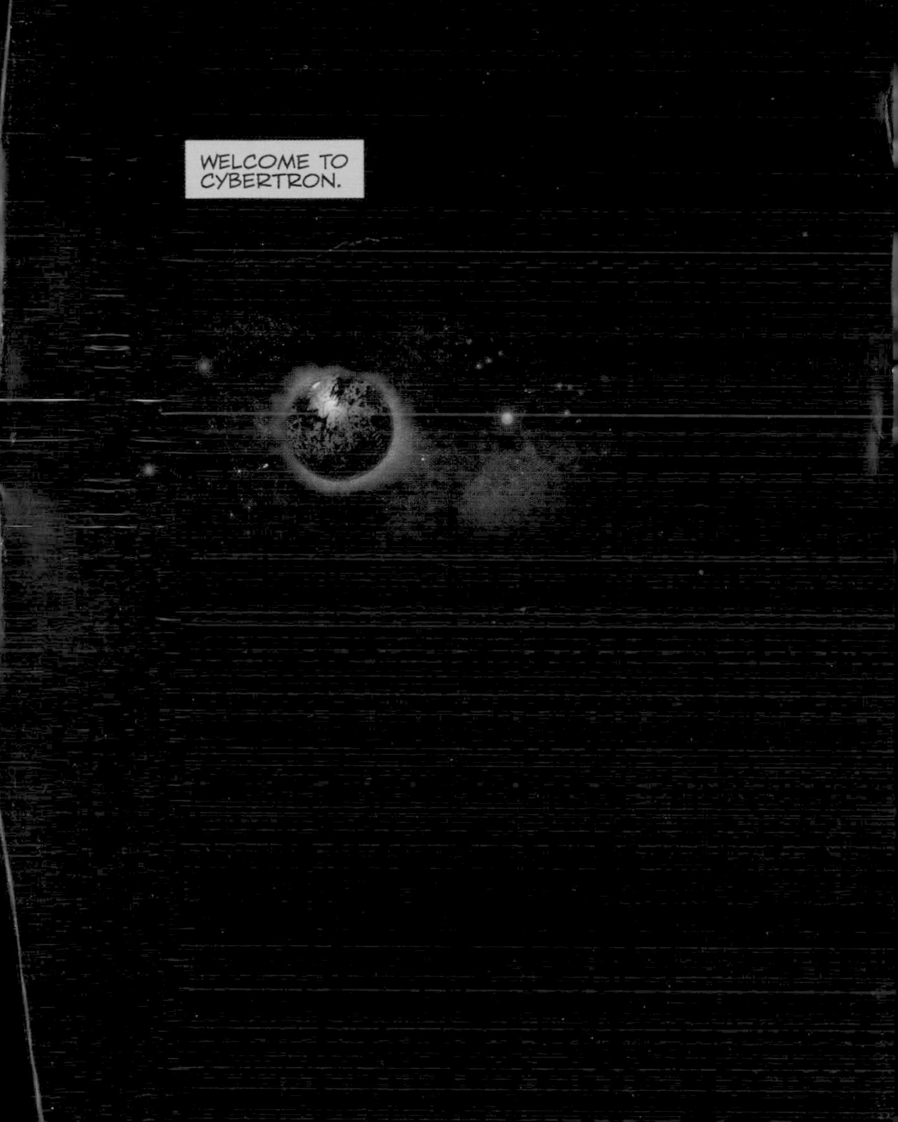
WELCOME TO CYBERTRON.

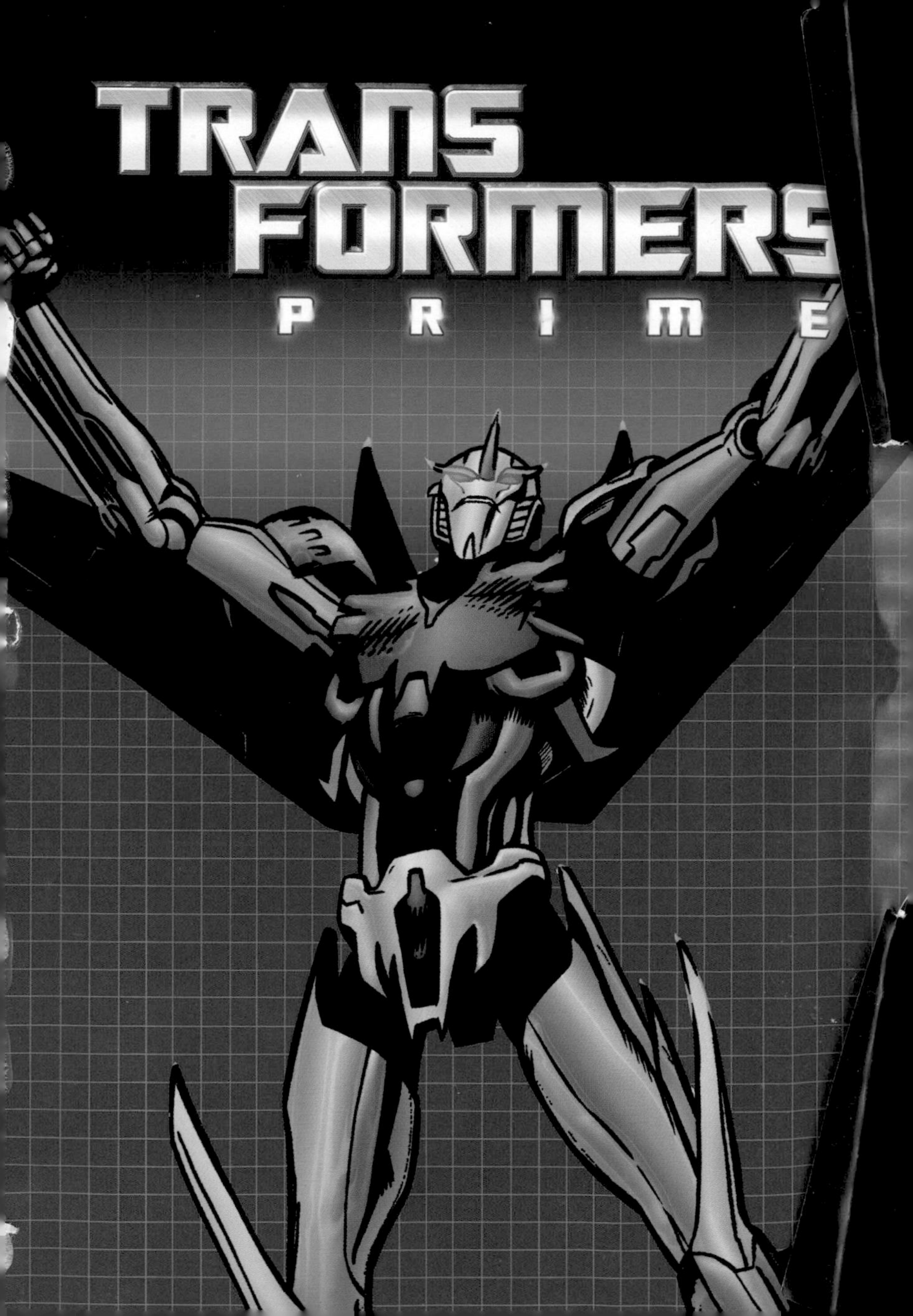
TRANS FORMERS
PRIME

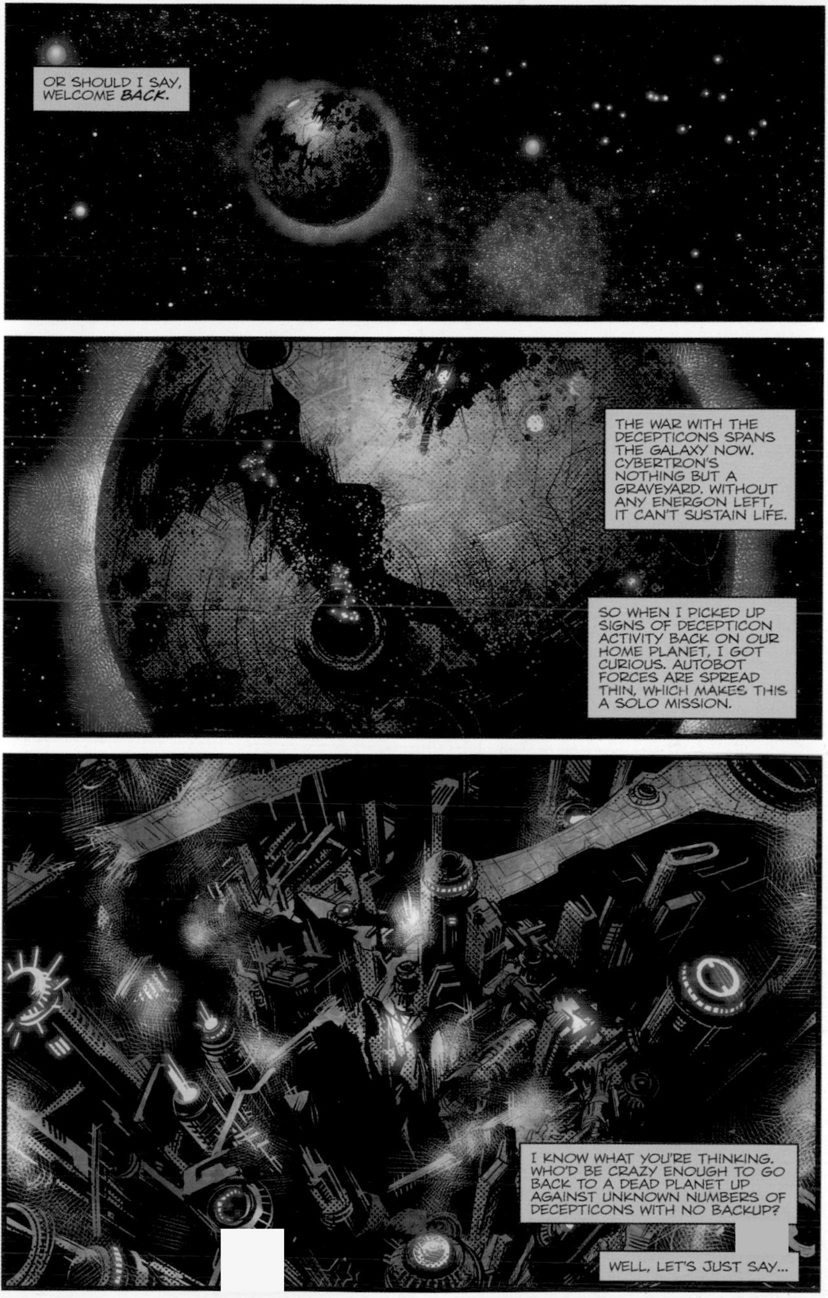
OR SHOULD I SAY, WELCOME *BACK*.
THE WAR WITH THE DECEPTICONS SPANS THE GALAXY NOW. CYBERTRON'S NOTHING BUT A GRAVEYARD. WITHOUT ANY ENERGON LEFT, IT CAN'T SUSTAIN LIFE.
SO WHEN I PICKED UP SIGNS OF DECEPTICON ACTIVITY BACK ON OUR HOME PLANET, I GOT CURIOUS. AUTOBOT FORCES ARE SPREAD THIN, WHICH MAKES THIS A SOLO MISSION.
I KNOW WHAT YOU'RE THINKING. WHO'D BE CRAZY ENOUGH TO GO BACK TO A DEAD PLANET UP AGAINST UNKNOWN NUMBERS OF DECEPTICONS WITH NO BACKUP?
WELL, LET'S JUST SAY...

...THEY DON'T CALL ME CLIFFJUMPER FOR NOTHING!
ZARK
KA-CHOOM
KA-CHOOM

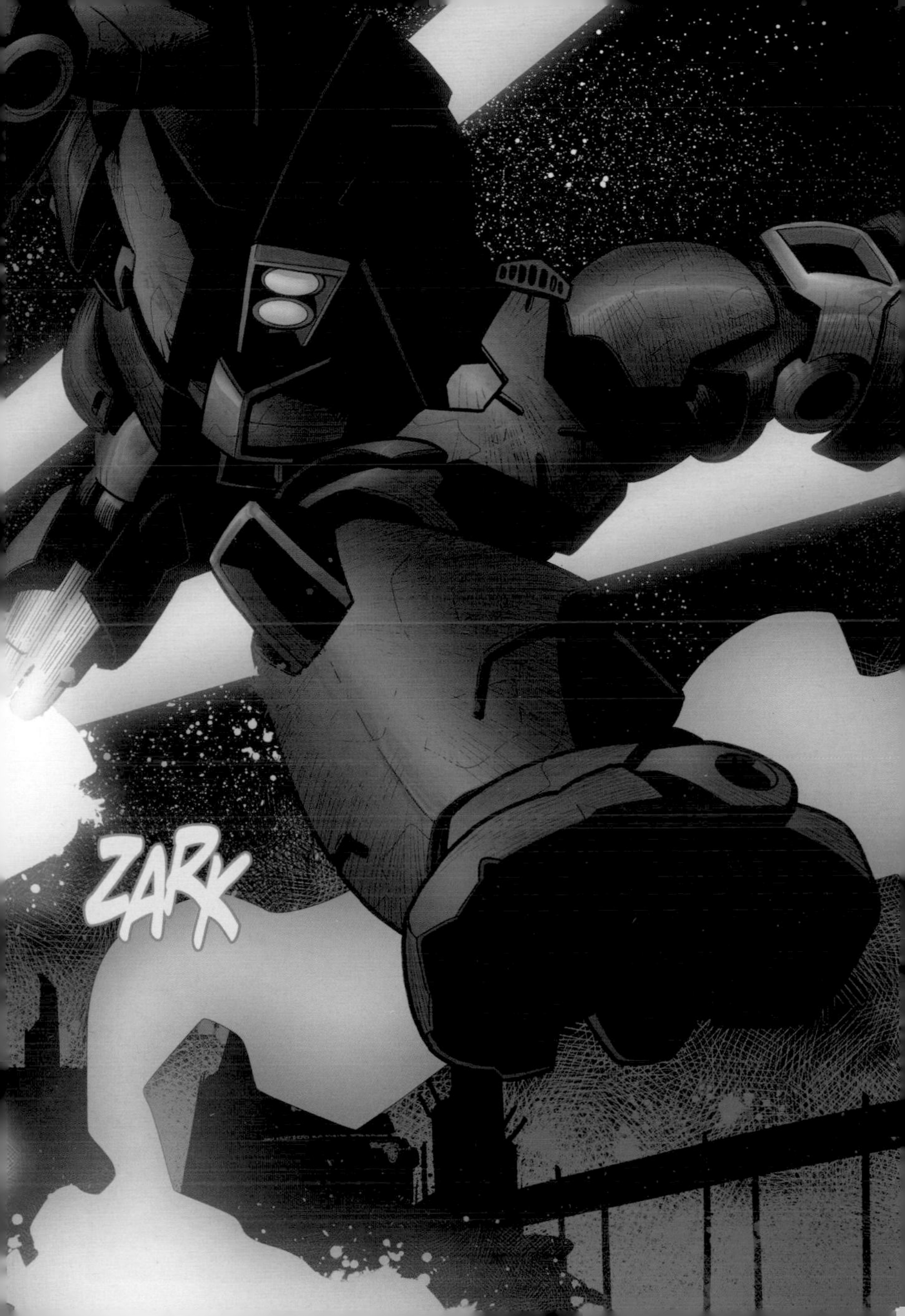
ZARK

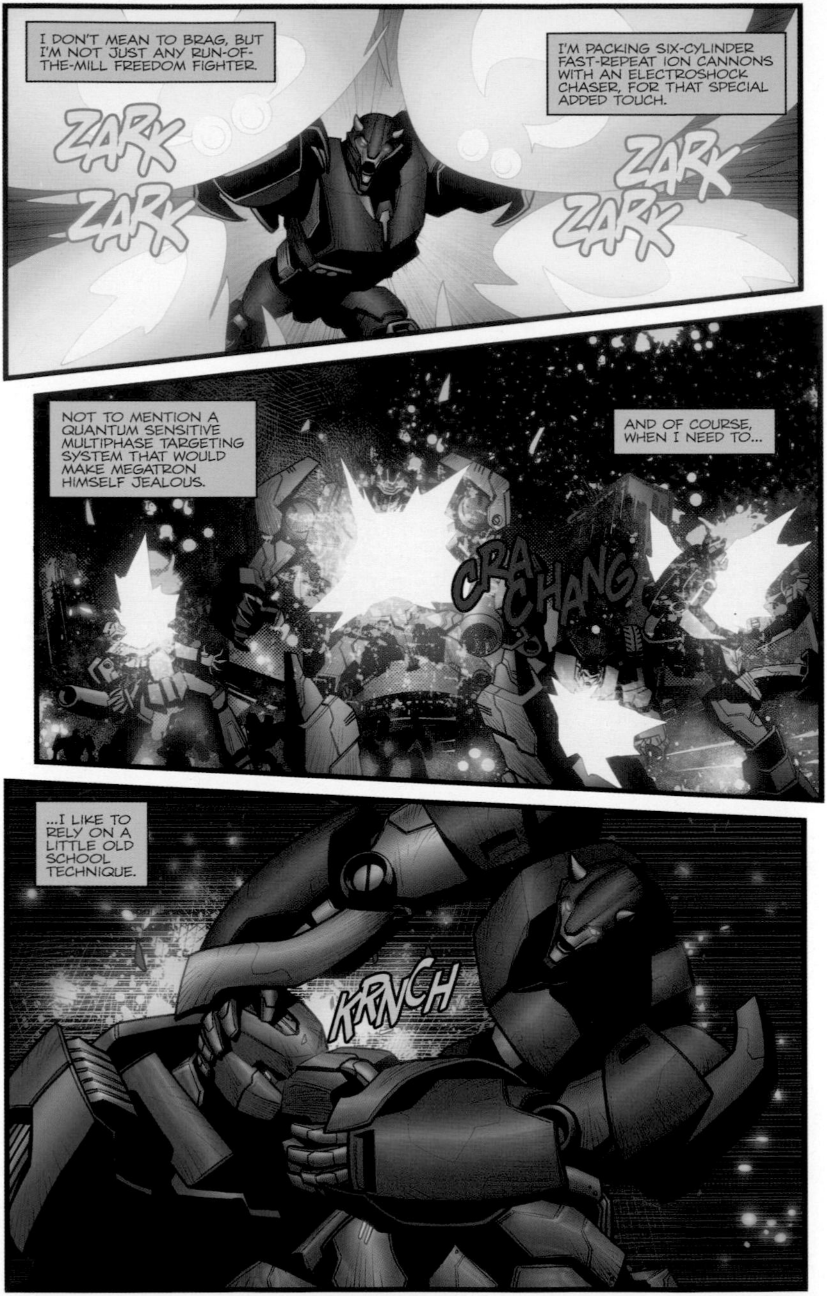
I DON'T MEAN TO BRAG, BUT I'M NOT JUST ANY RUN-OF-THE-MILL FREEDOM FIGHTER.
I'M PACKING SIX-CYLINDER FAST-REPEAT ION CANNONS WITH AN ELECTROSHOCK CHASER, FOR THAT SPECIAL ADDED TOUCH.
ZARK
ZARK
ZARK
ZARK
NOT TO MENTION A QUANTUM SENSITIVE MULTIPHASE TARGETING SYSTEM THAT WOULD MAKE MEGATRON HIMSELF JEALOUS.
AND OF COURSE, WHEN I NEED TO...
CRA-CHANG
...I LIKE TO RELY ON A LITTLE OLD SCHOOL TECHNIQUE.
KRNCH

I WAS HOPING THIS WOULD BE A QUICK TRIP–YOUR BASIC SMASH N' GRAB.
ZARK
AS IN, SMASH A FEW 'CONS, GRAB THE INTEL ON WHATEVER THEY'RE UP TO.
STILL...
...WHO DOESN'T LIKE A NICE LITTLE FIREFIGHT TO LIVEN UP THE DAY?
MISSED ME!
BRAK
BOOM

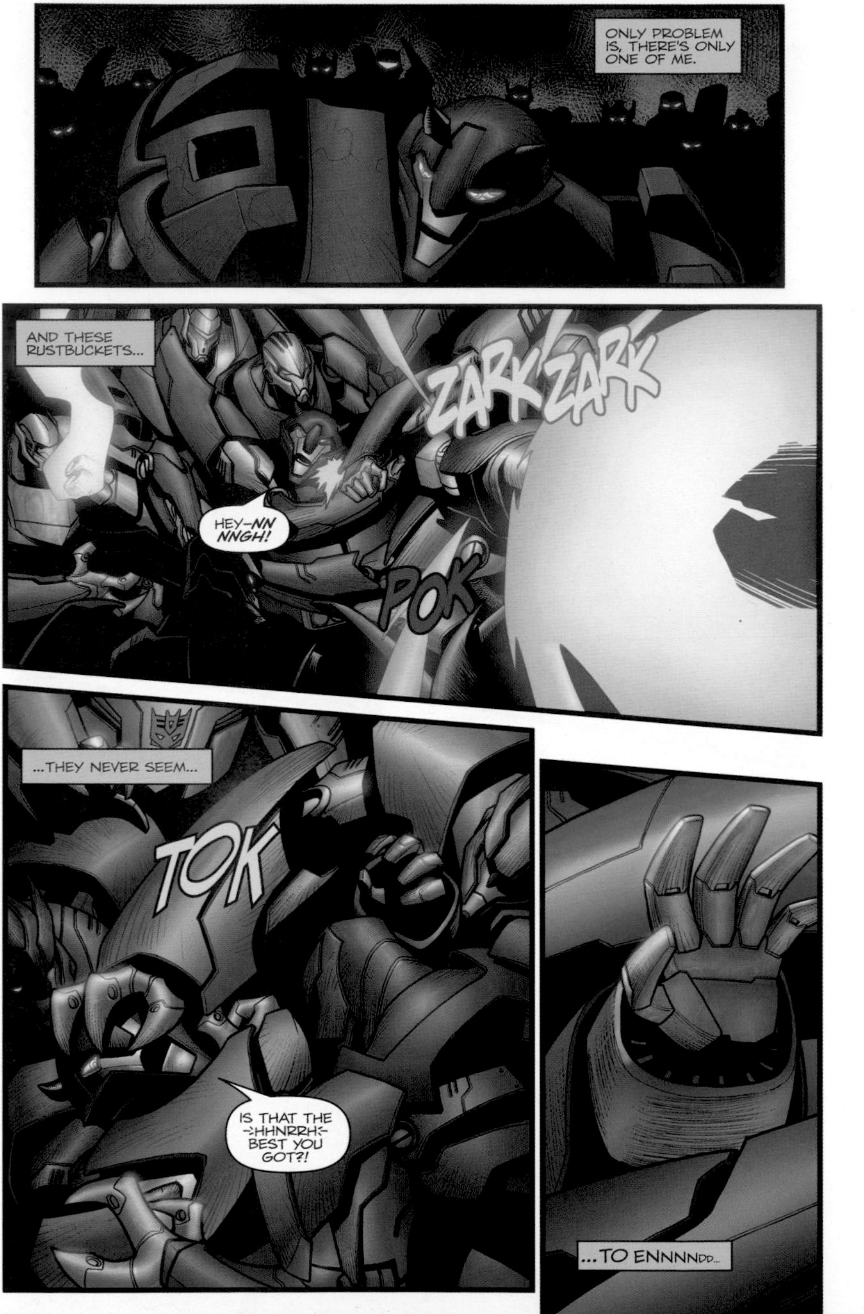
ONLY PROBLEM IS, THERE'S ONLY ONE OF ME.
AND THESE RUSTBUCKETS...
ZARK ZARK
HEY--NN NNGH!
POK
...THEY NEVER SEEM...
TOK
IS THAT THE --HHNRRH-- BEST YOU GOT?!
...TO ENNNNDD...

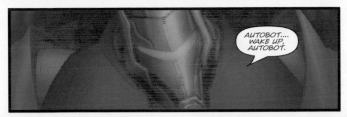

AUTOBOT....
WAKE UP,
AUTOBOT.

WAKE UP!
I WANT TO
SHOW YOU
SOMETHING!

WELCOME TO
YOUR NEW HOME!
AT LEAST IT WILL
BE, FOR THE SHORT
REMAINDER OF
YOUR MISERABLE
EXISTENCE!

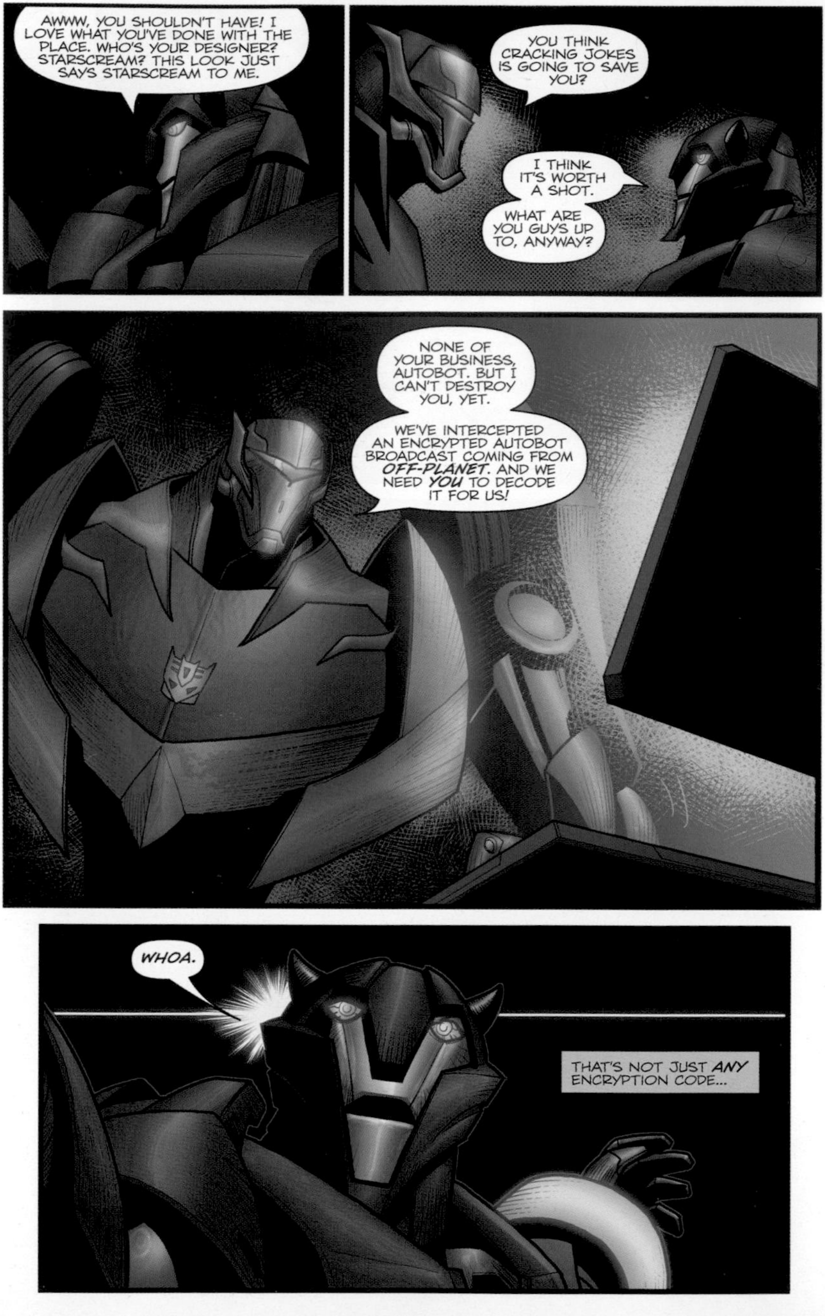
AWWW, YOU SHOULDN'T HAVE! I LOVE WHAT YOU'VE DONE WITH THE PLACE. WHO'S YOUR DESIGNER? STARSCREAM? THIS LOOK JUST SAYS STARSCREAM TO ME.
YOU THINK CRACKING JOKES IS GOING TO SAVE YOU?
I THINK IT'S WORTH A SHOT.
WHAT ARE YOU GUYS UP TO, ANYWAY?
NONE OF YOUR BUSINESS, AUTOBOT. BUT I CAN'T DESTROY YOU, YET.
WE'VE INTERCEPTED AN ENCRYPTED AUTOBOT BROADCAST COMING FROM OFF-PLANET. AND WE NEED YOU TO DECODE IT FOR US!
WHOA.
THAT'S NOT JUST ANY ENCRYPTION CODE...

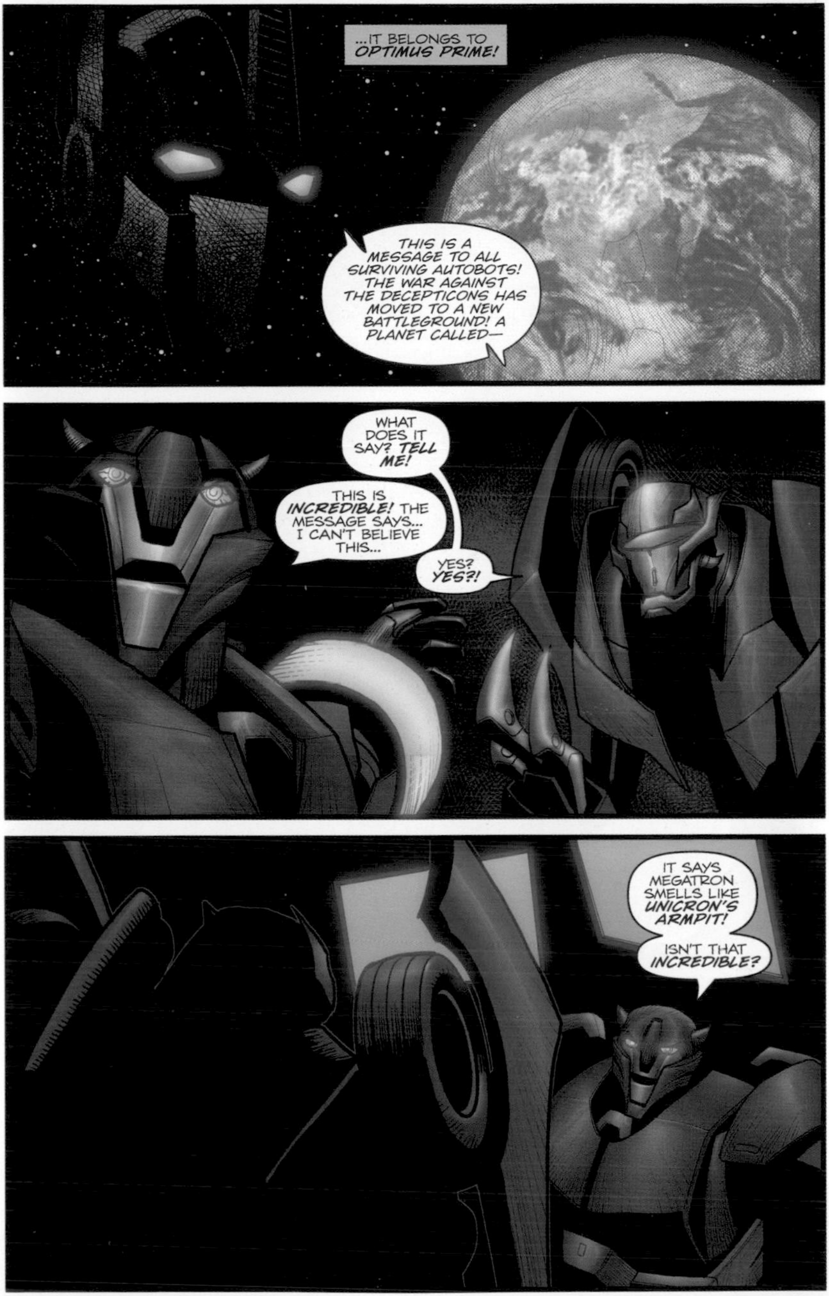
...IT BELONGS TO OPTIMUS PRIME!
THIS IS A MESSAGE TO ALL SURVIVING AUTOBOTS! THE WAR AGAINST THE DECEPTICONS HAS MOVED TO A NEW BATTLEGROUND! A PLANET CALLED—
WHAT DOES IT SAY? TELL ME!
THIS IS INCREDIBLE! THE MESSAGE SAYS... I CAN'T BELIEVE THIS...
YES? YES?!
IT SAYS MEGATRON SMELLS LIKE UNICRON'S ARMPIT!
ISN'T THAT INCREDIBLE?

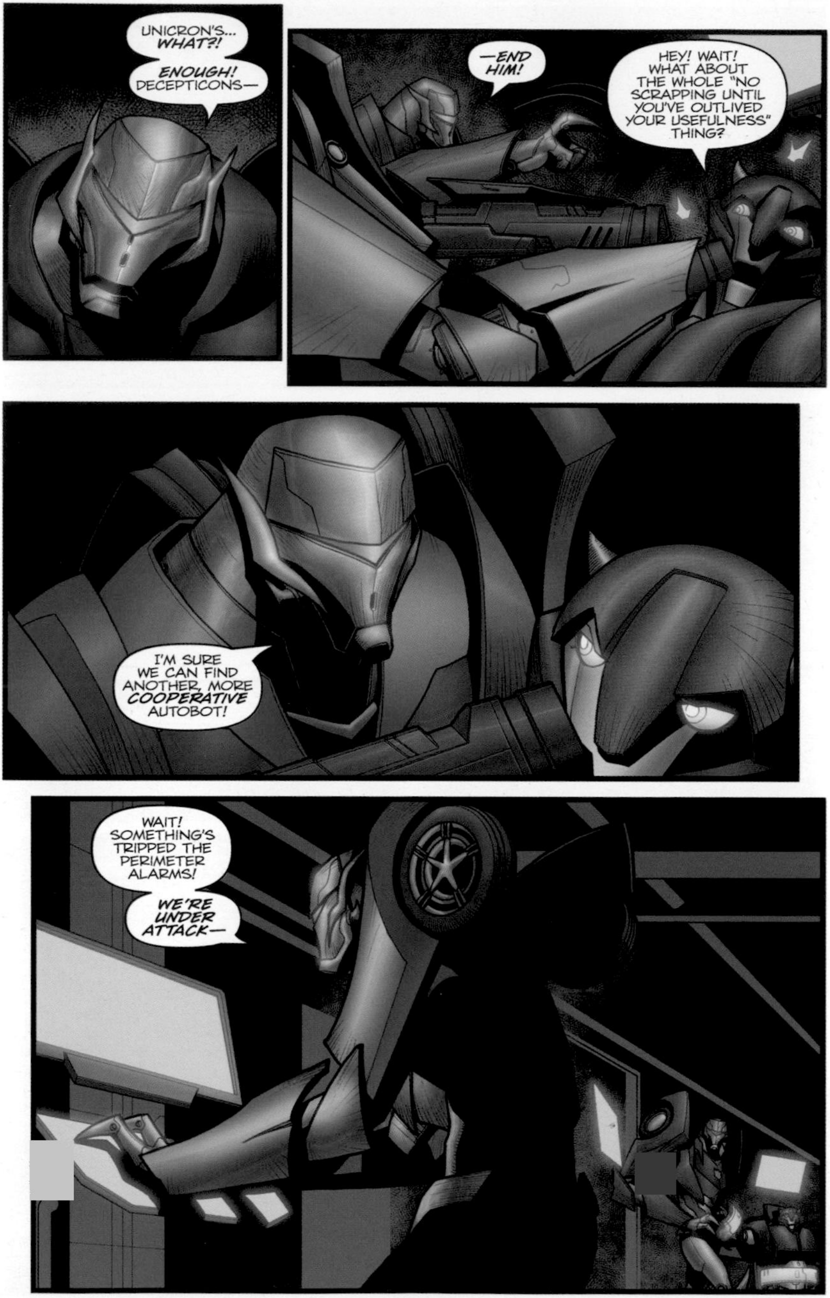
UNICRON'S... WHAT?!
ENOUGH! DECEPTICONS—
—END HIM!
HEY! WAIT! WHAT ABOUT THE WHOLE "NO SCRAPPING UNTIL YOU'VE OUTLIVED YOUR USEFULNESS" THING?
I'M SURE WE CAN FIND ANOTHER, MORE COOPERATIVE AUTOBOT!
WAIT! SOMETHING'S TRIPPED THE PERIMETER ALARMS!
WE'RE UNDER ATTACK—

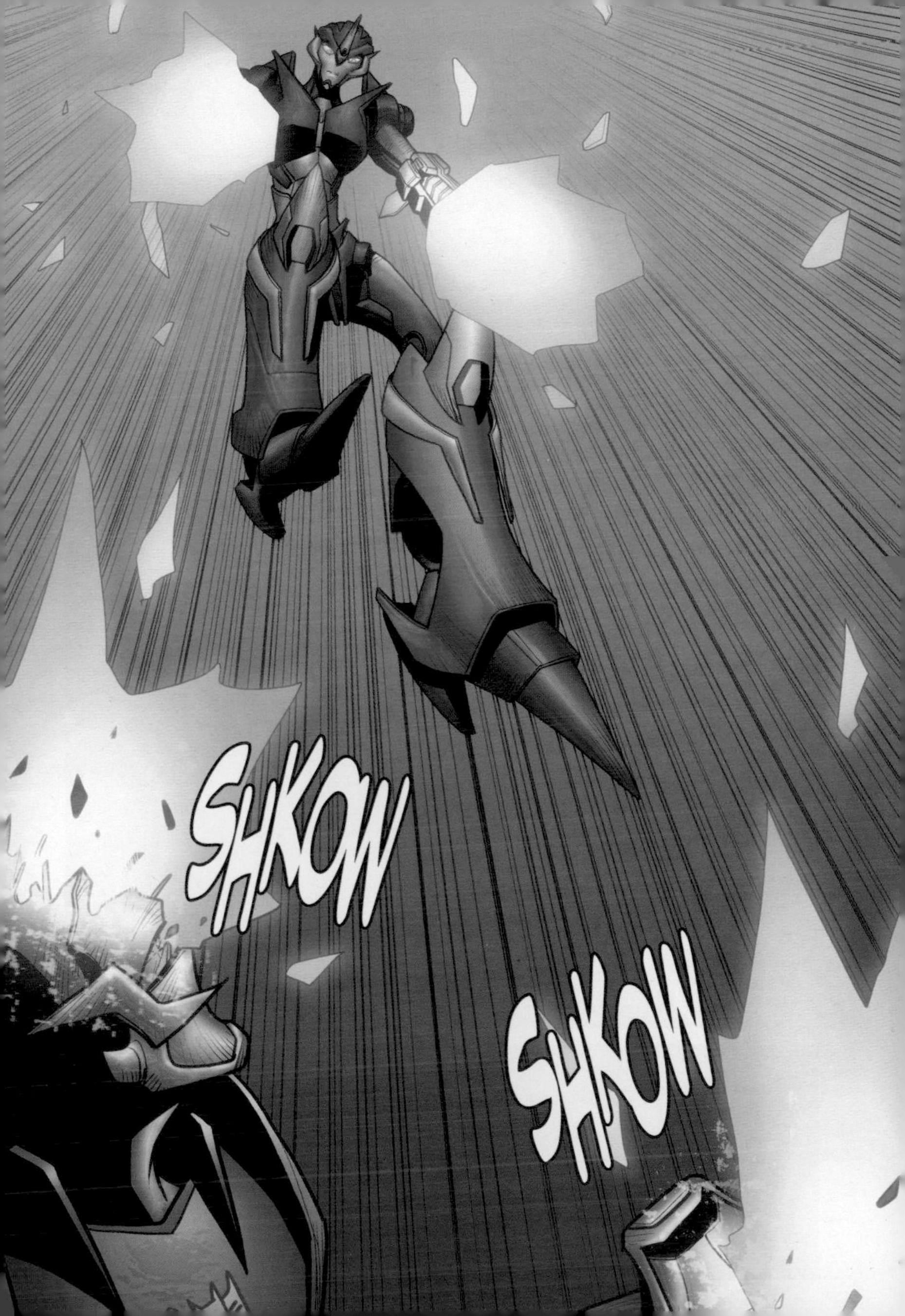
SHKOW
SHKOW

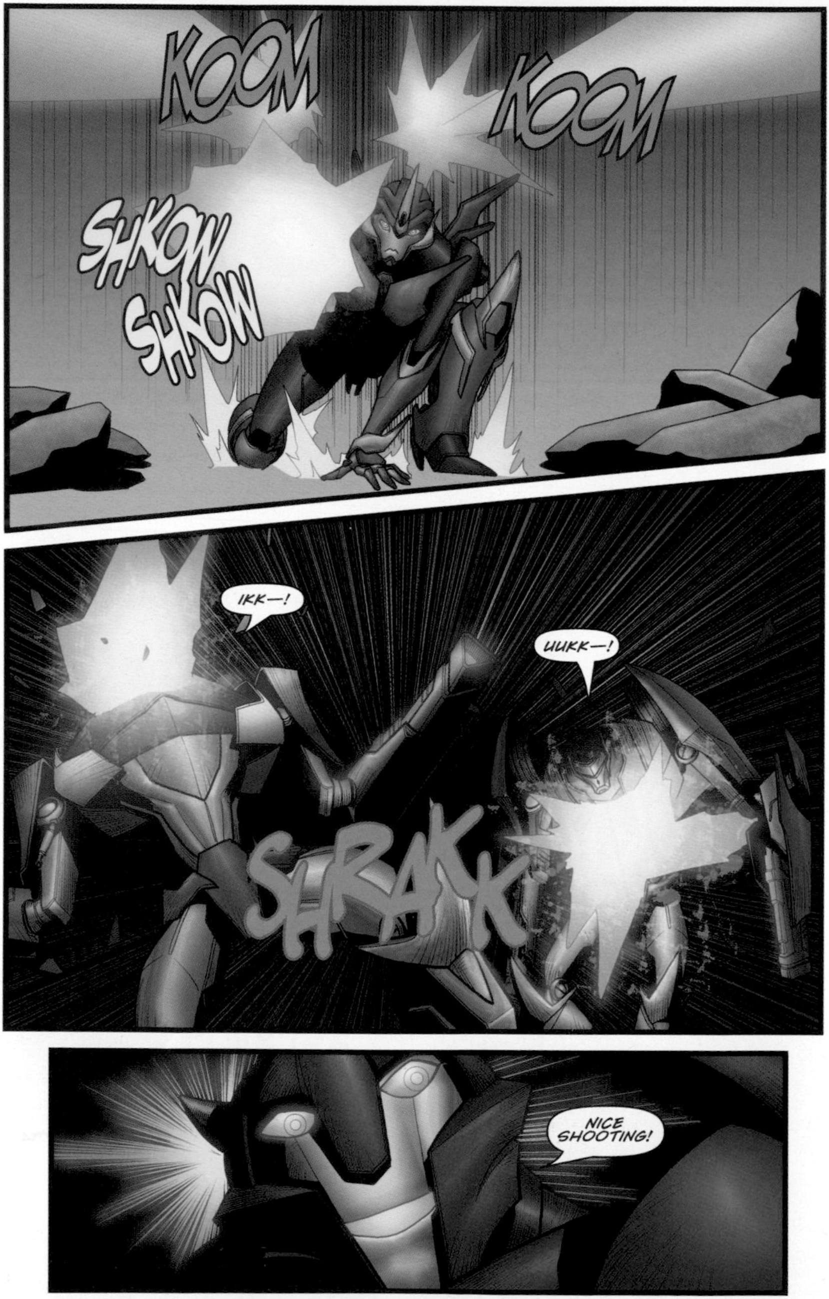
KOOM
KOOM
SHKOW
SHKOW
SHKOW
IKK—!
UUKK—!
SHRAKK
NICE SHOOTING!

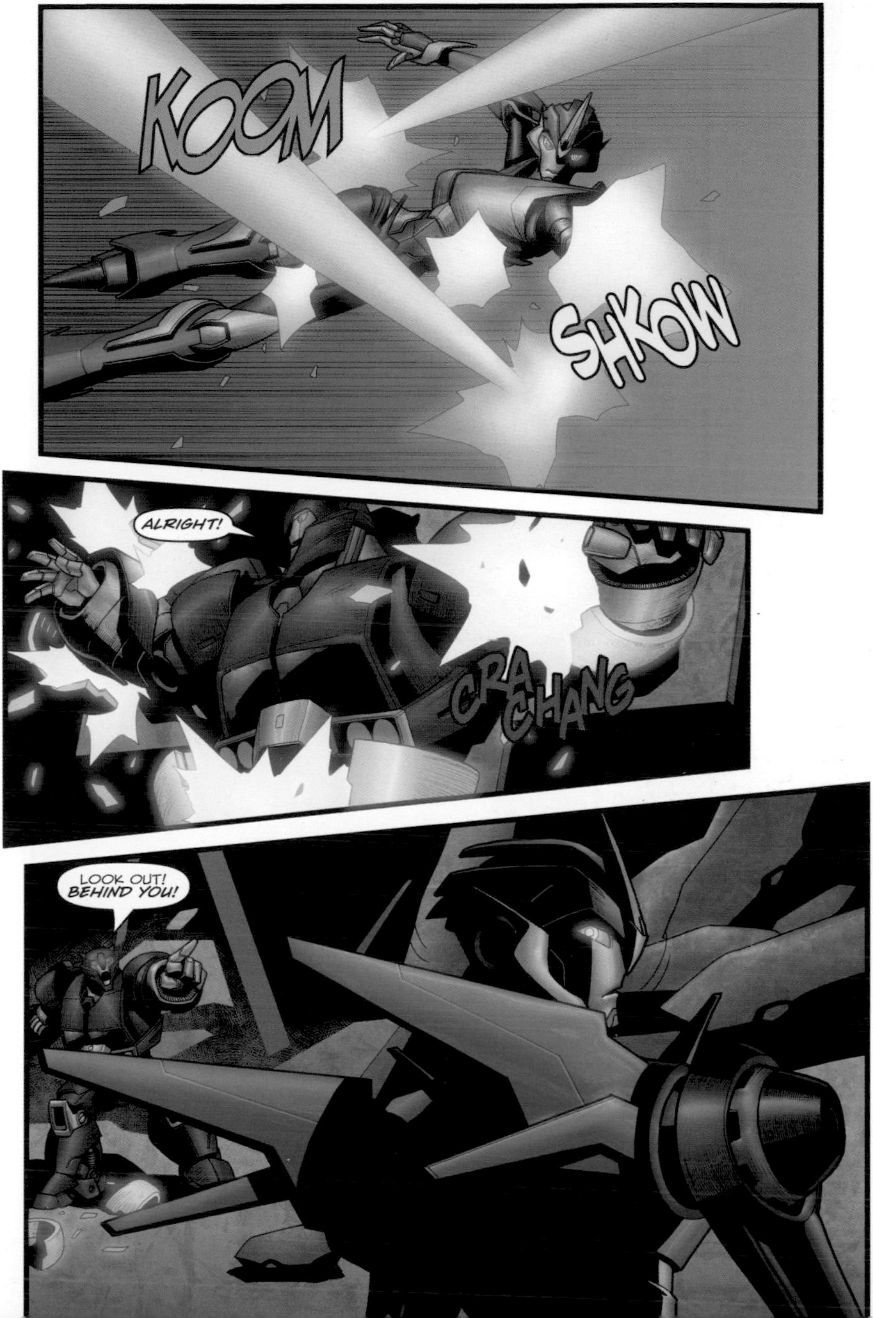
KOOM
SHKOW
ALRIGHT!
CRA CHANG
LOOK OUT! BEHIND YOU!

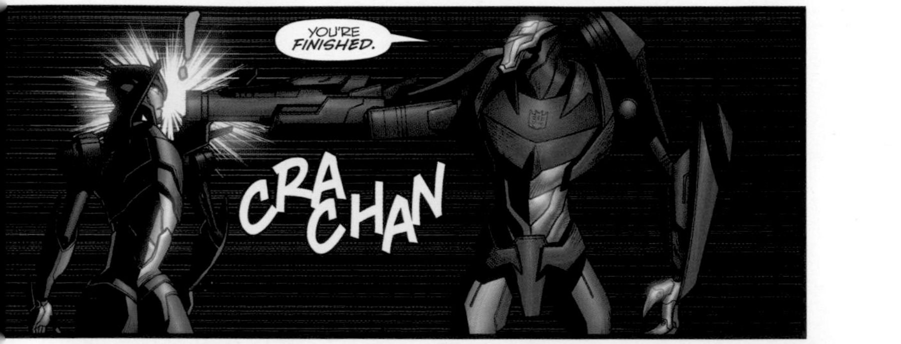
!
YOU'RE FINISHED.
CRA CHAN
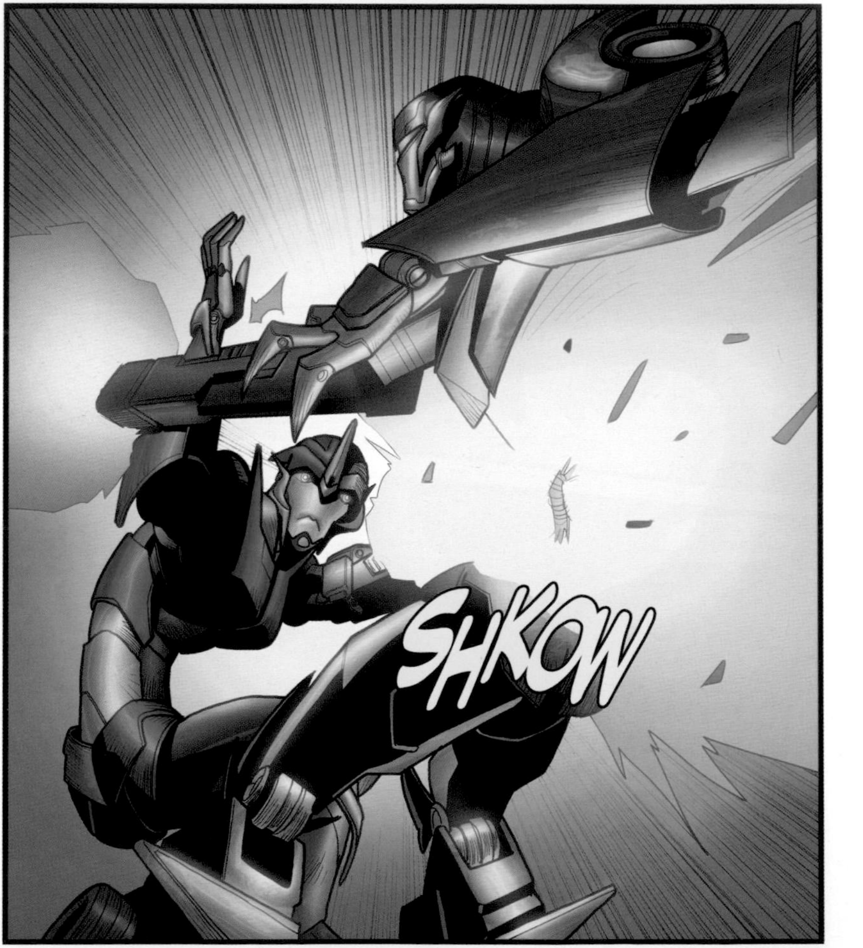
SHKOW

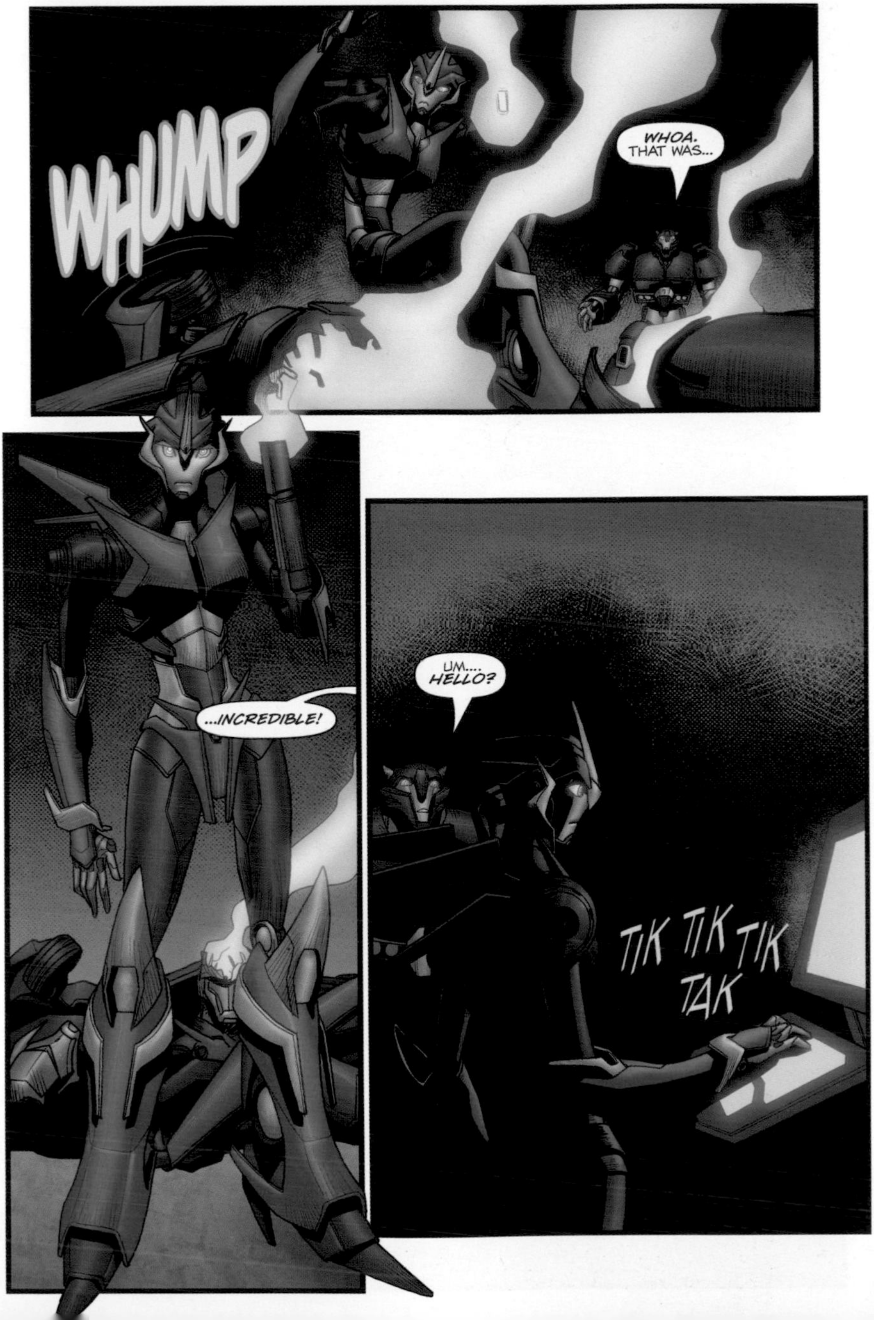
WHUMP
WHOA. THAT WAS...
...INCREDIBLE!
UM.... HELLO?
TIK TIK TIK TIK TAK

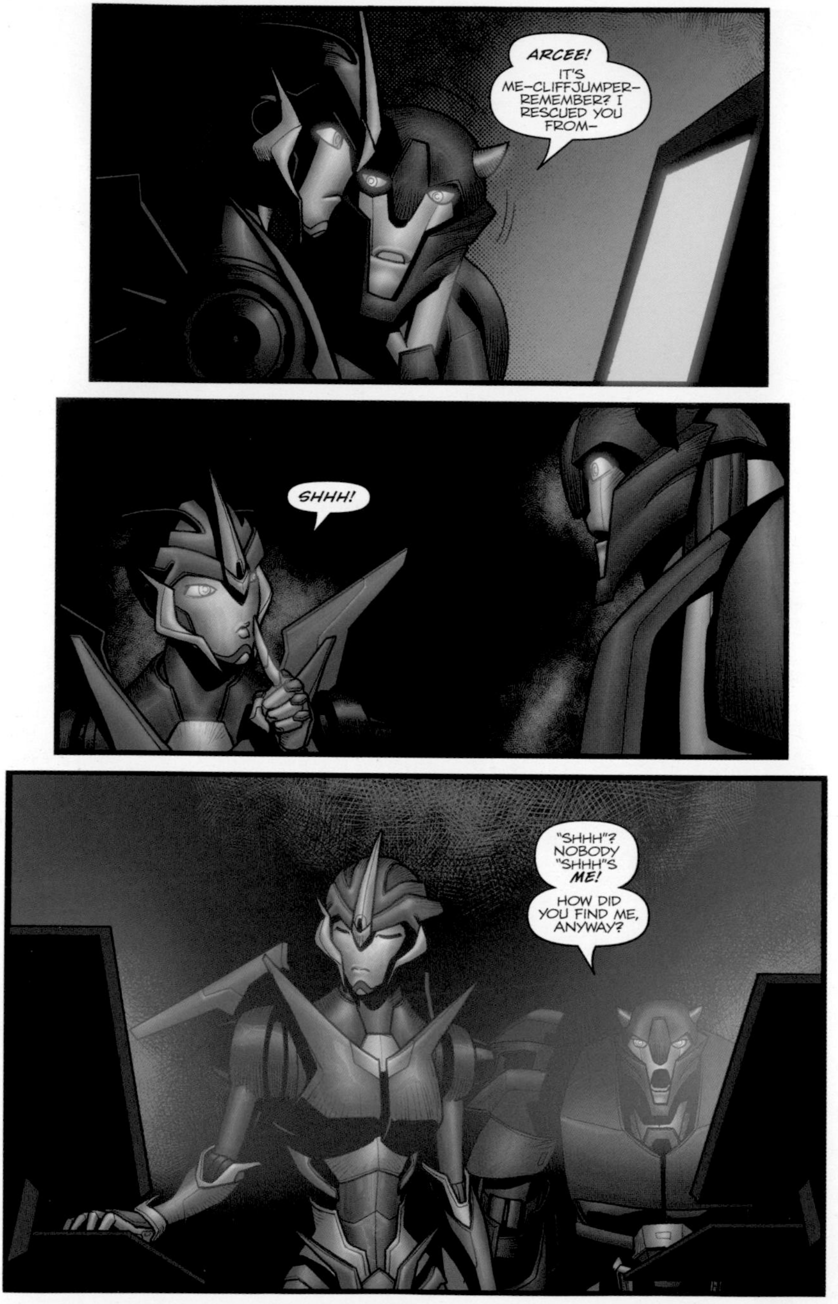
ARCEE!
IT'S ME—CLIFFJUMPER—REMEMBER? I RESCUED YOU FROM—
SHHH!
"SHHH"? NOBODY "SHHH"S ME!
HOW DID YOU FIND ME, ANYWAY?

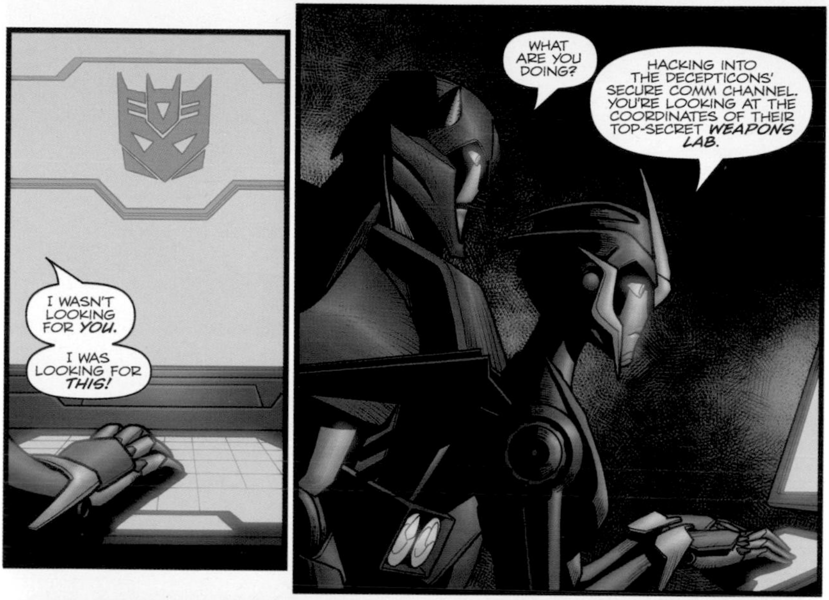
I WASN'T LOOKING FOR YOU.
I WAS LOOKING FOR THIS!
WHAT ARE YOU DOING?
HACKING INTO THE DECEPTICONS' SECURE COMM CHANNEL. YOU'RE LOOKING AT THE COORDINATES OF THEIR TOP-SECRET WEAPONS LAB.

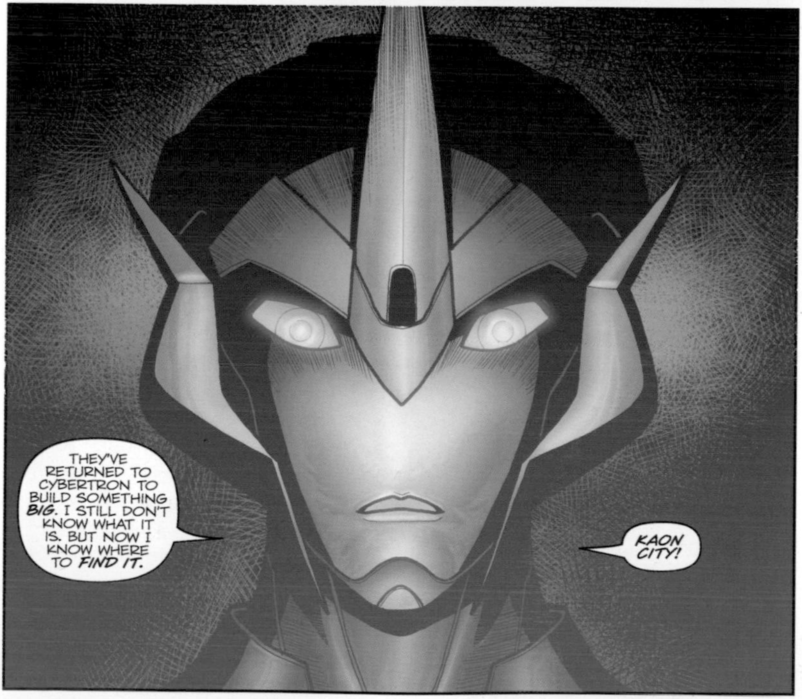
THEY'VE RETURNED TO CYBERTRON TO BUILD SOMETHING BIG. I STILL DON'T KNOW WHAT IT IS. BUT NOW I KNOW WHERE TO FIND IT.
KAON CITY!

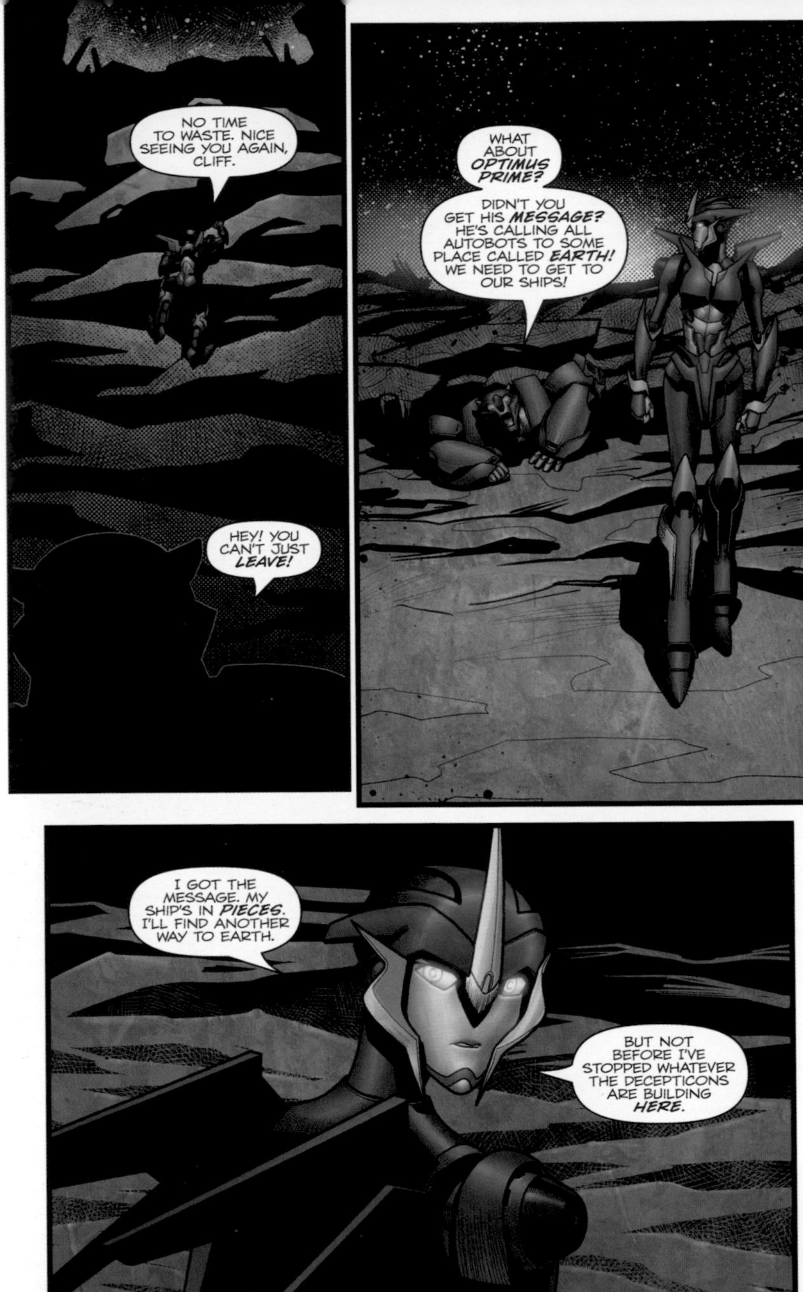
NO TIME TO WASTE. NICE SEEING YOU AGAIN, CLIFF.
HEY! YOU CAN'T JUST LEAVE!
WHAT ABOUT OPTIMUS PRIME?
DIDN'T YOU GET HIS MESSAGE? HE'S CALLING ALL AUTOBOTS TO SOME PLACE CALLED EARTH! WE NEED TO GET TO OUR SHIPS!
I GOT THE MESSAGE. MY SHIP'S IN PIECES. I'LL FIND ANOTHER WAY TO EARTH.
BUT NOT BEFORE I'VE STOPPED WHATEVER THE DECEPTICONS ARE BUILDING HERE.

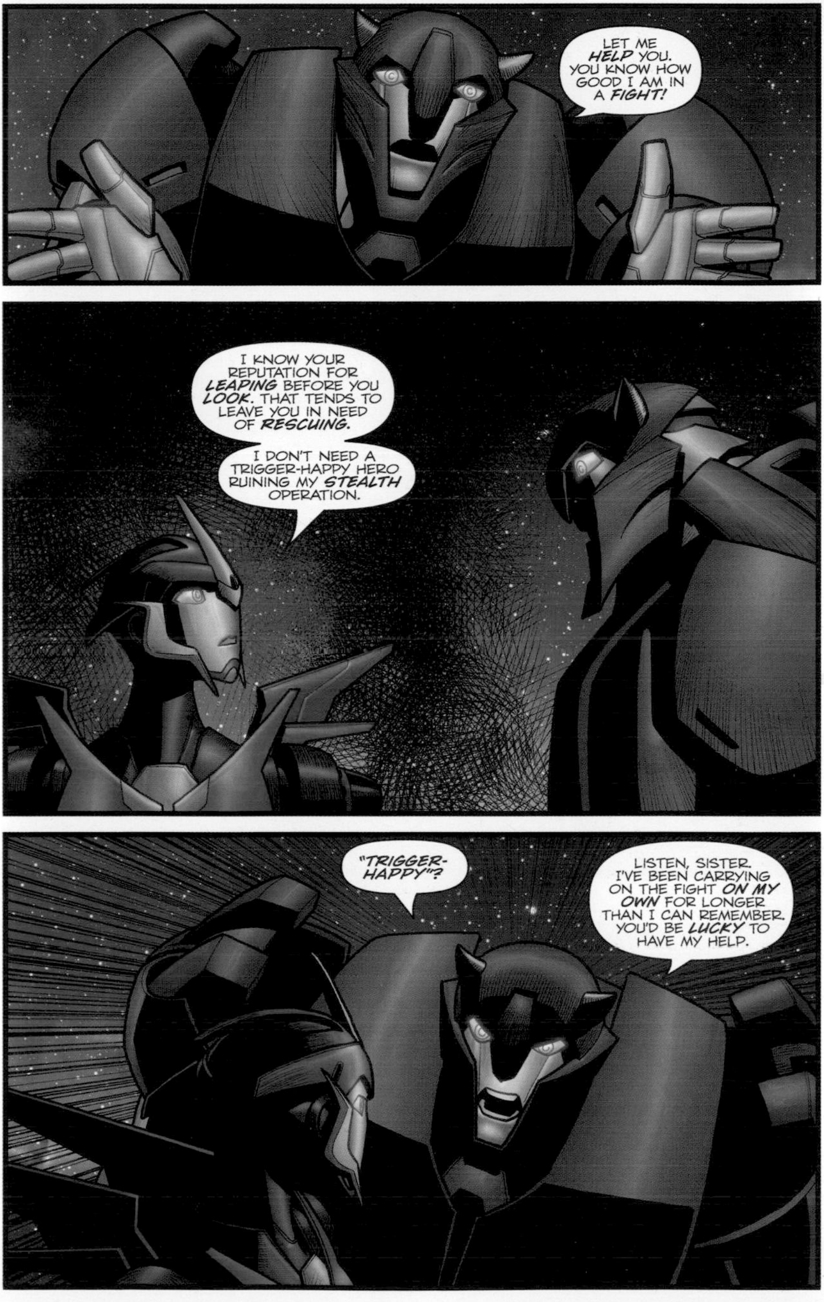
LET ME HELP YOU. YOU KNOW HOW GOOD I AM IN A FIGHT!
I KNOW YOUR REPUTATION FOR LEAPING BEFORE YOU LOOK. THAT TENDS TO LEAVE YOU IN NEED OF RESCUING.
I DON'T NEED A TRIGGER-HAPPY HERO RUINING MY STEALTH OPERATION.
"TRIGGER-HAPPY"?
LISTEN, SISTER. I'VE BEEN CARRYING ON THE FIGHT ON MY OWN FOR LONGER THAN I CAN REMEMBER. YOU'D BE LUCKY TO HAVE MY HELP.

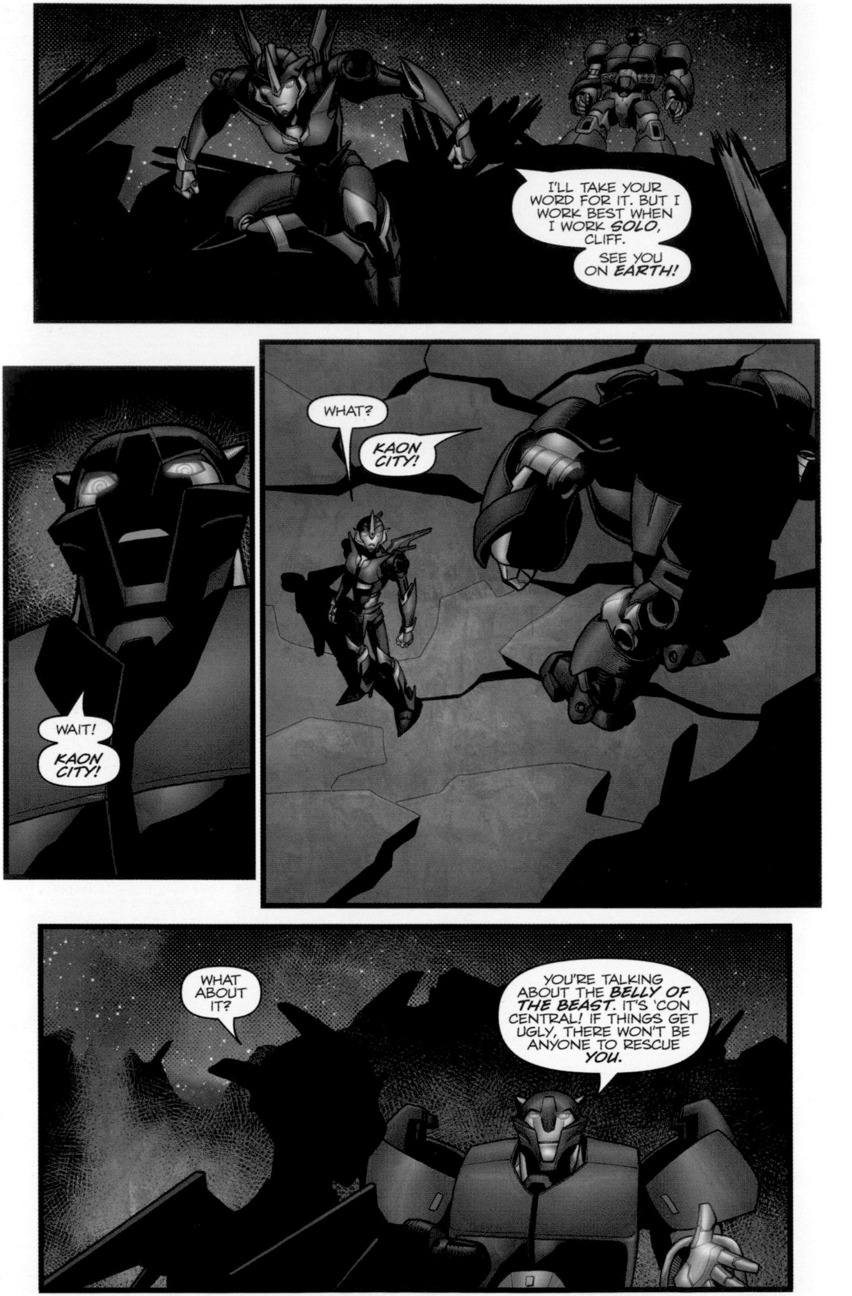
I'LL TAKE YOUR WORD FOR IT. BUT I WORK BEST WHEN I WORK SOLO, CLIFF.
SEE YOU ON EARTH!
WAIT!
KAON CITY!
WHAT?
KAON CITY!
WHAT ABOUT IT?
YOU'RE TALKING ABOUT THE BELLY OF THE BEAST. IT'S 'CON CENTRAL! IF THINGS GET UGLY, THERE WON'T BE ANYONE TO RESCUE YOU.

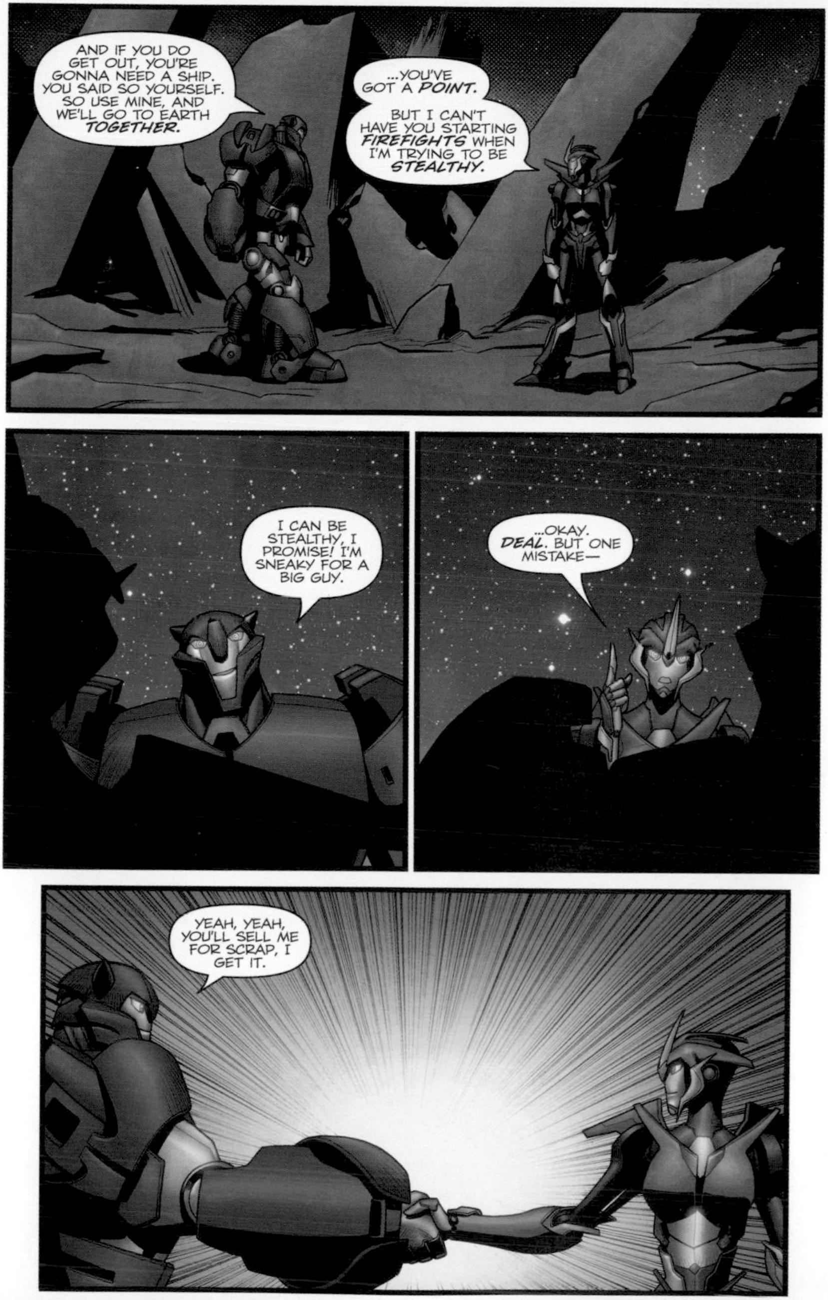
AND IF YOU DO GET OUT, YOU'RE GONNA NEED A SHIP. YOU SAID SO YOURSELF. SO USE MINE, AND WE'LL GO TO EARTH **TOGETHER.**
...YOU'VE GOT A **POINT.**
BUT I CAN'T HAVE YOU STARTING **FIREFIGHTS** WHEN I'M TRYING TO BE **STEALTHY.**
I CAN BE STEALTHY, I PROMISE! I'M SNEAKY FOR A BIG GUY.
...OKAY. **DEAL.** BUT ONE MISTAKE—
YEAH, YEAH, YOU'LL SELL ME FOR SCRAP, I GET IT.

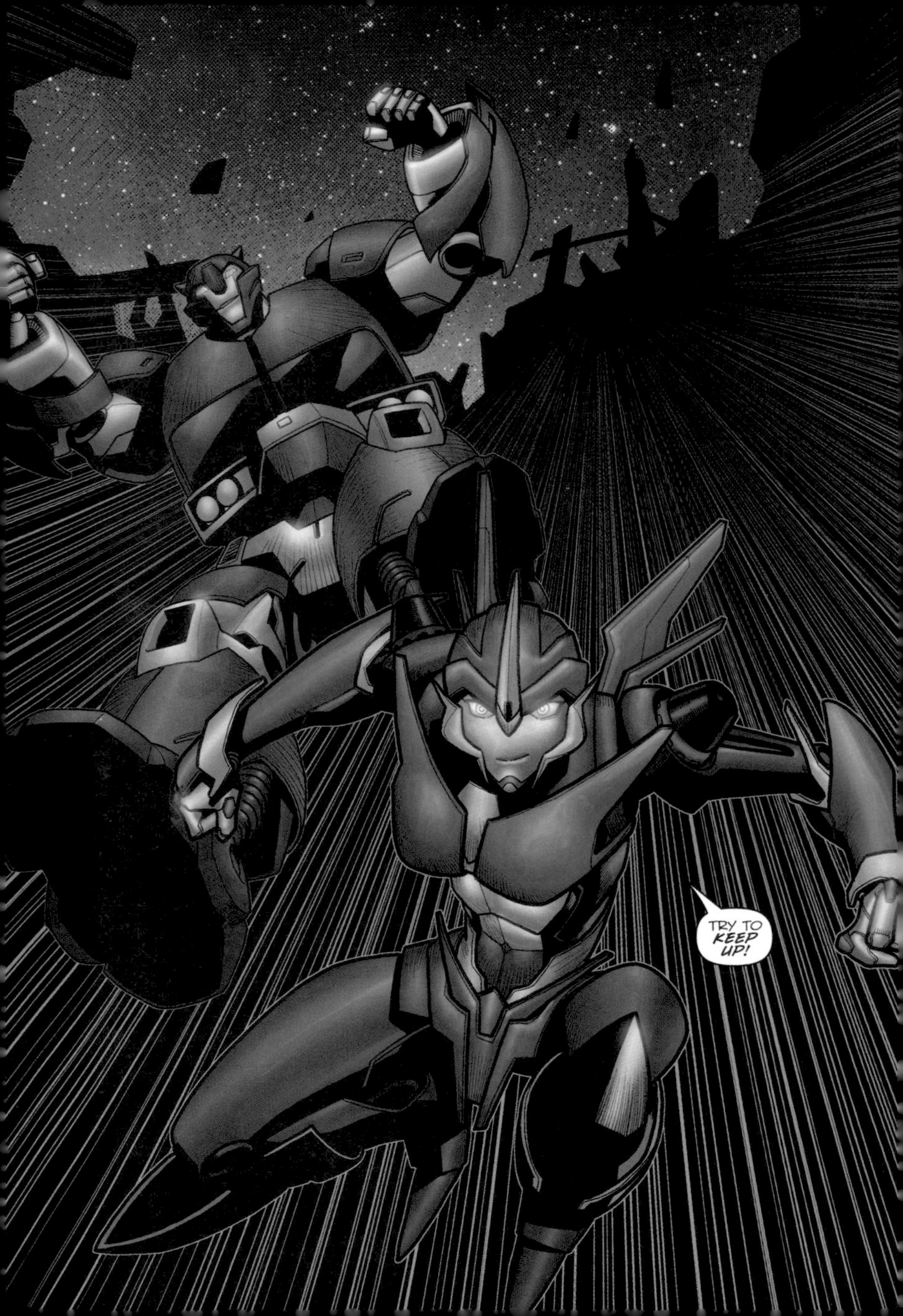
TRY TO KEEP UP!

Chapter Two

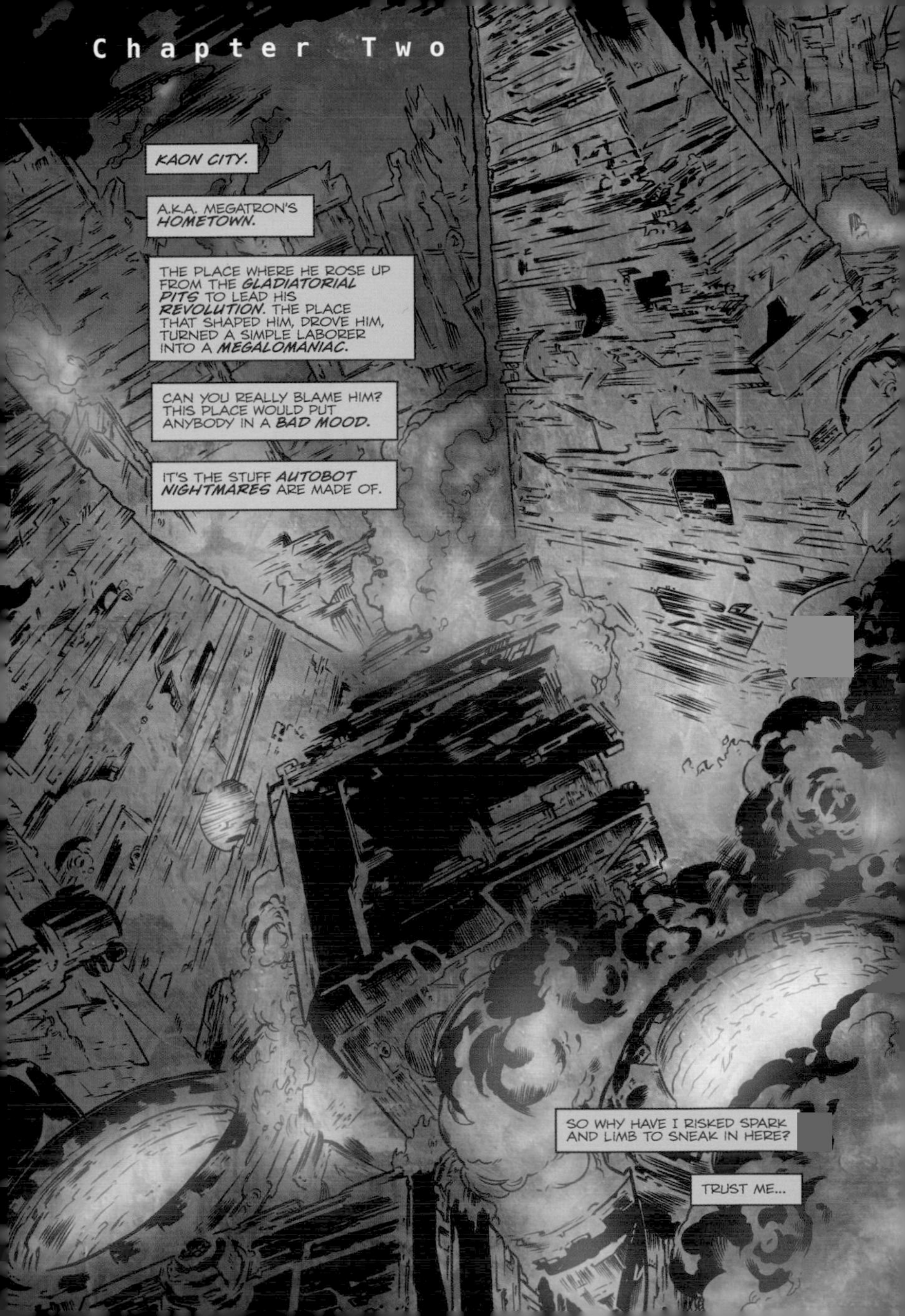
KAON CITY.
A.K.A. MEGATRON'S HOMETOWN.
THE PLACE WHERE HE ROSE UP FROM THE GLADIATORIAL PITS TO LEAD HIS REVOLUTION. THE PLACE THAT SHAPED HIM, DROVE HIM, TURNED A SIMPLE LABORER INTO A MEGALOMANIAC.
CAN YOU REALLY BLAME HIM? THIS PLACE WOULD PUT ANYBODY IN A BAD MOOD.
IT'S THE STUFF AUTOBOT NIGHTMARES ARE MADE OF.
SO WHY HAVE I RISKED SPARK AND LIMB TO SNEAK IN HERE?
TRUST ME...

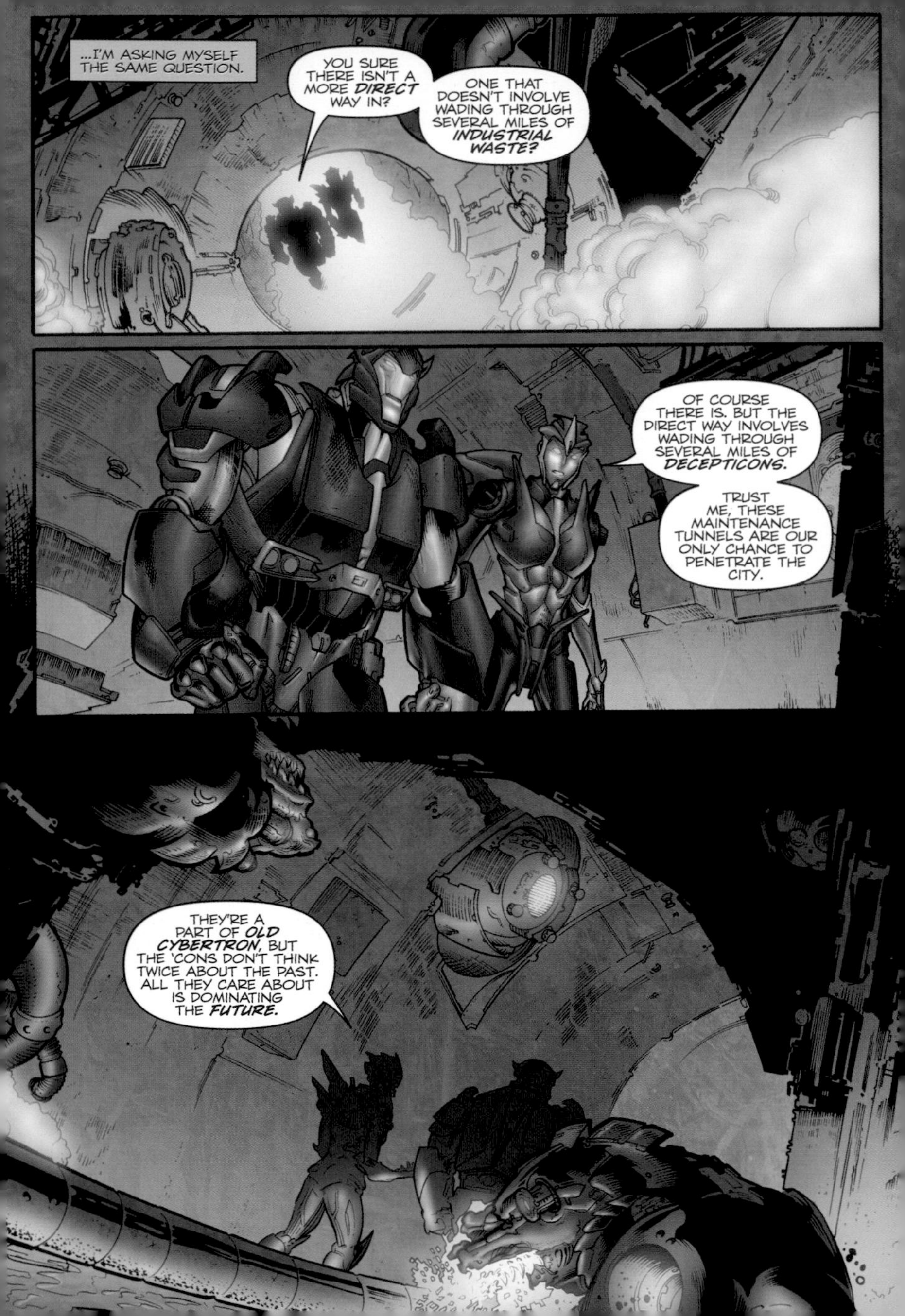

...I'M ASKING MYSELF THE SAME QUESTION.
YOU SURE THERE ISN'T A MORE *DIRECT* WAY IN?
ONE THAT DOESN'T INVOLVE WADING THROUGH SEVERAL MILES OF *INDUSTRIAL WASTE?*
OF COURSE THERE IS. BUT THE DIRECT WAY INVOLVES WADING THROUGH SEVERAL MILES OF *DECEPTICONS.*
TRUST ME, THESE MAINTENANCE TUNNELS ARE OUR ONLY CHANCE TO PENETRATE THE CITY.
THEY'RE A PART OF *OLD CYBERTRON,* BUT THE 'CONS DON'T THINK TWICE ABOUT THE PAST. ALL THEY CARE ABOUT IS DOMINATING THE *FUTURE.*

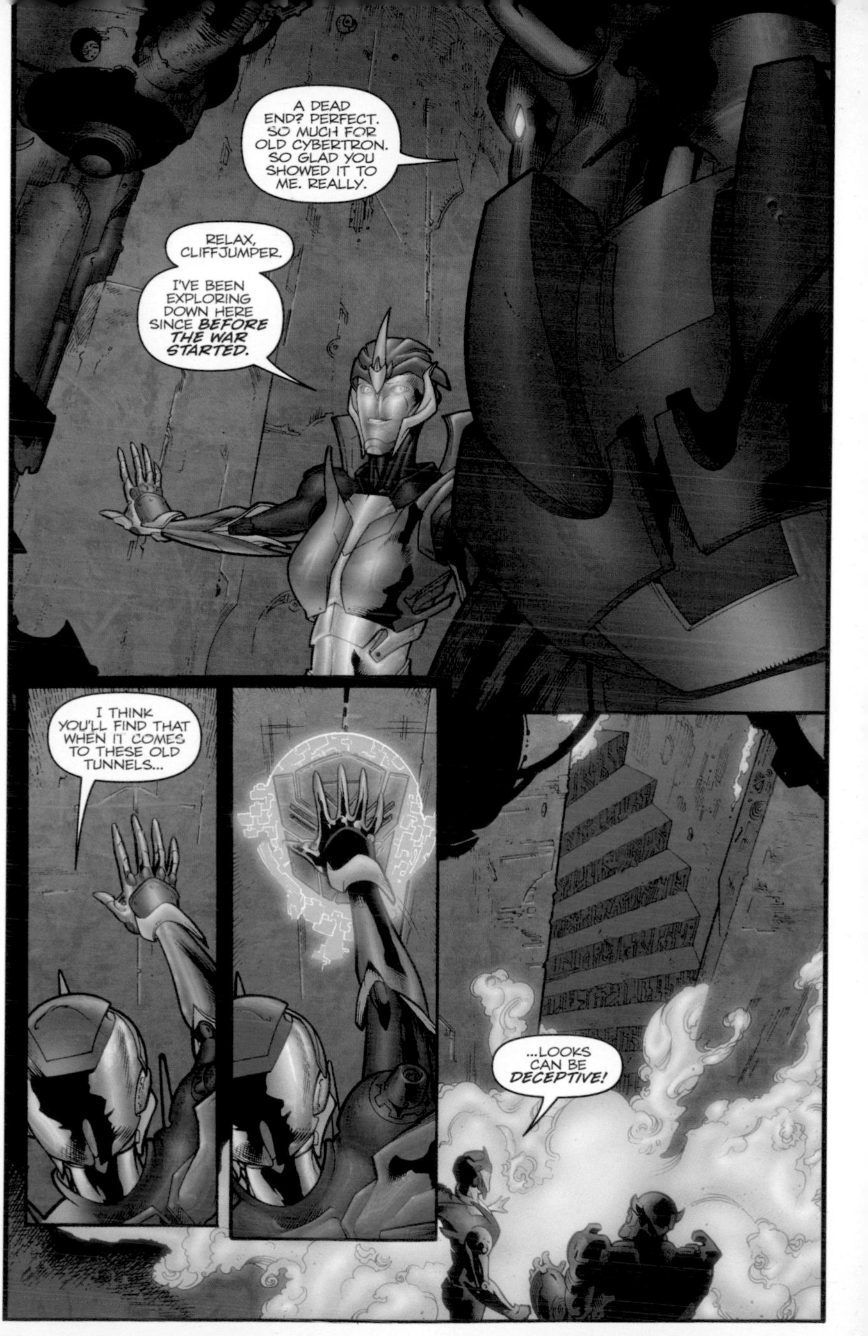

A DEAD END? PERFECT. SO MUCH FOR OLD CYBERTRON. SO GLAD YOU SHOWED IT TO ME. REALLY.
RELAX, CLIFFJUMPER.
I'VE BEEN EXPLORING DOWN HERE SINCE *BEFORE THE WAR STARTED.*
I THINK YOU'LL FIND THAT WHEN IT COMES TO THESE OLD TUNNELS...
...LOOKS CAN BE *DECEPTIVE!*

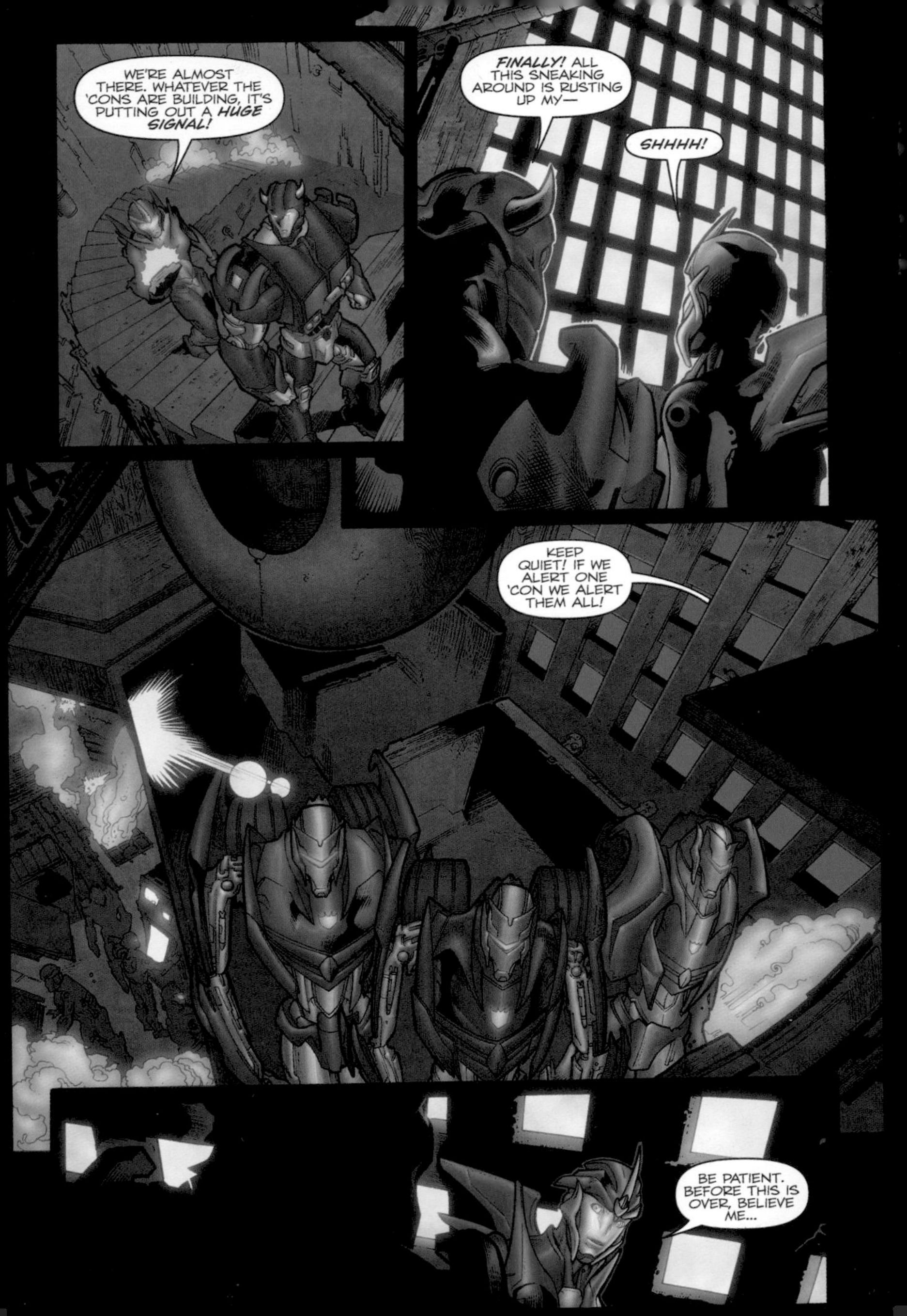
WE'RE ALMOST THERE. WHATEVER THE 'CONS ARE BUILDING, IT'S PUTTING OUT A HUGE SIGNAL!
FINALLY! ALL THIS SNEAKING AROUND IS RUSTING UP MY—
SHHHH!
KEEP QUIET! IF WE ALERT ONE 'CON WE ALERT THEM ALL!
BE PATIENT. BEFORE THIS IS OVER, BELIEVE ME...

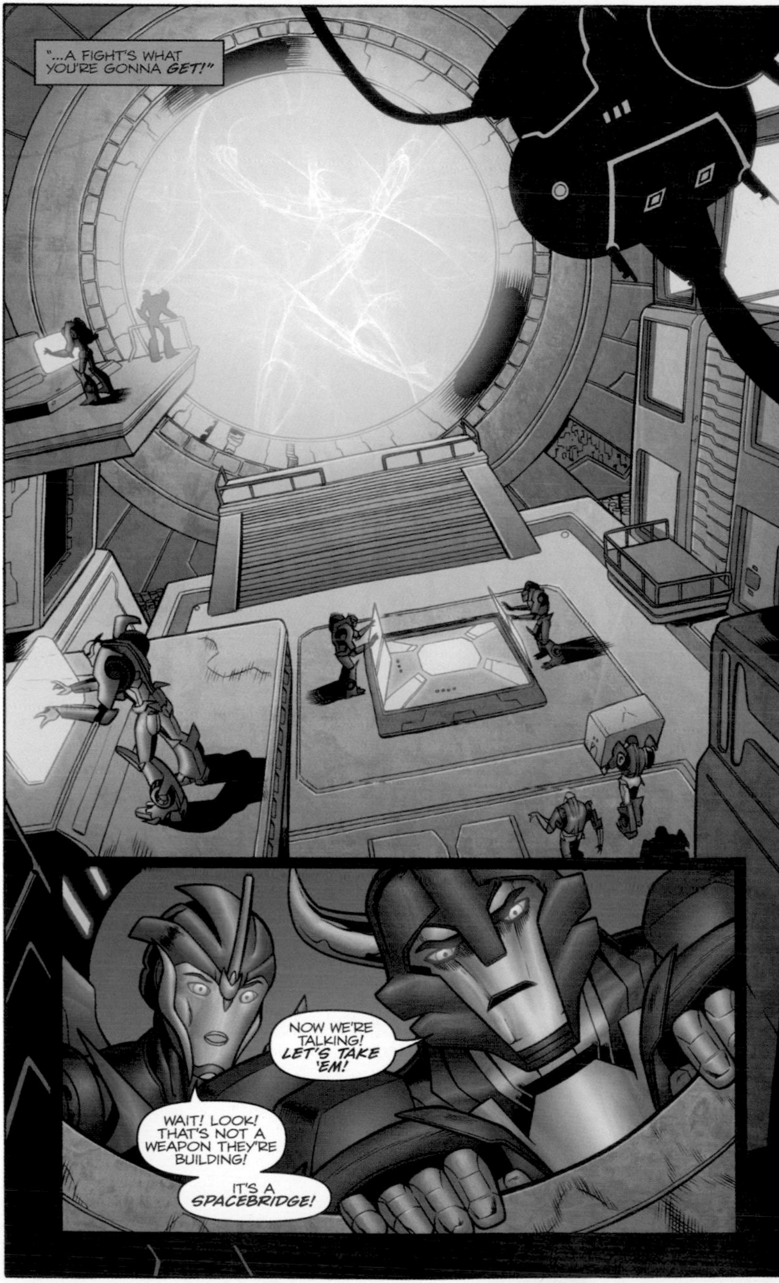
"...A FIGHT'S WHAT YOU'RE GONNA GET!"
NOW WE'RE TALKING! LET'S TAKE 'EM!
WAIT! LOOK! THAT'S NOT A WEAPON THEY'RE BUILDING!
IT'S A SPACEBRIDGE!

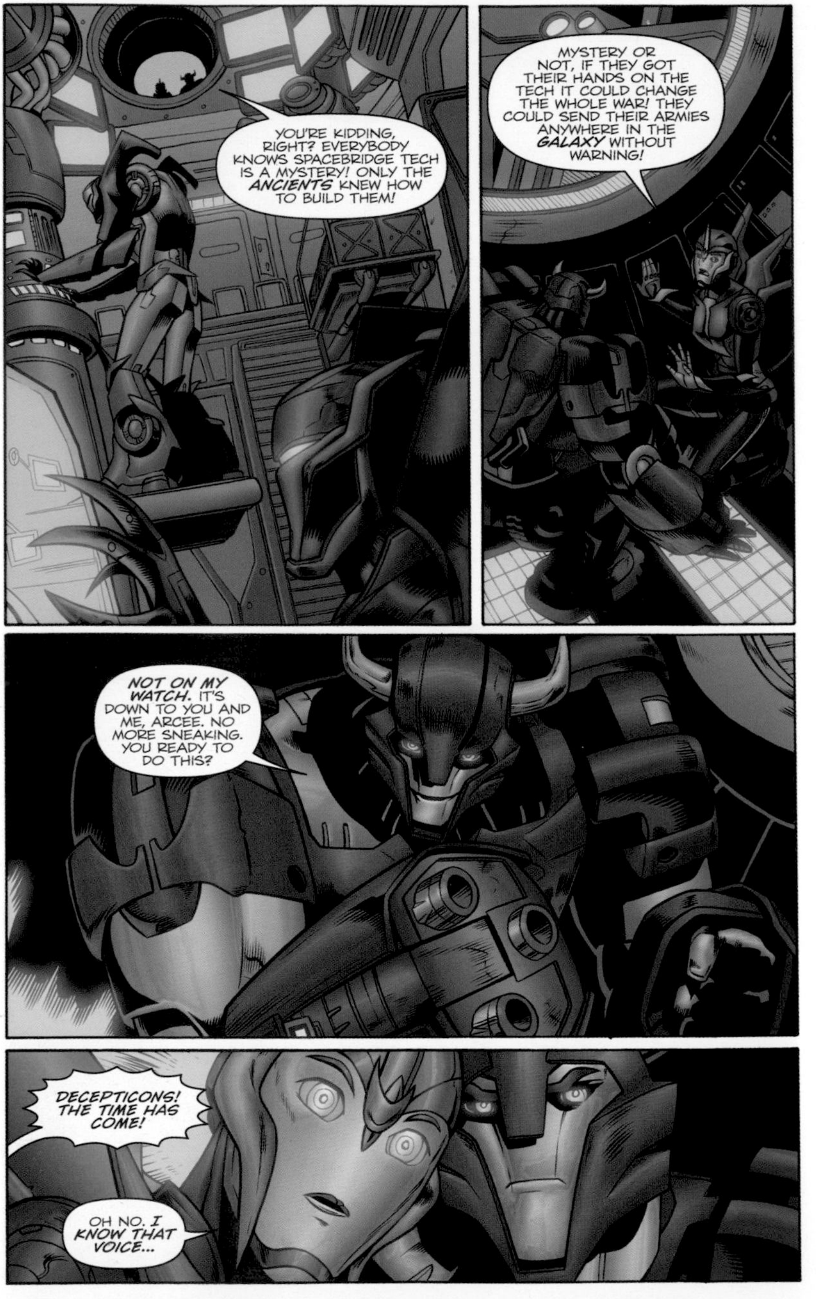
YOU'RE KIDDING, RIGHT? EVERYBODY KNOWS SPACEBRIDGE TECH IS A MYSTERY! ONLY THE *ANCIENTS* KNEW HOW TO BUILD THEM!
MYSTERY OR NOT, IF THEY GOT THEIR HANDS ON THE TECH IT COULD CHANGE THE WHOLE WAR! THEY COULD SEND THEIR ARMIES ANYWHERE IN THE *GALAXY* WITHOUT WARNING!
NOT ON MY WATCH. IT'S DOWN TO YOU AND ME, ARCEE. NO MORE SNEAKING. YOU READY TO DO THIS?
DECEPTICONS! THE TIME HAS COME!
OH NO. *I KNOW THAT* VOICE...

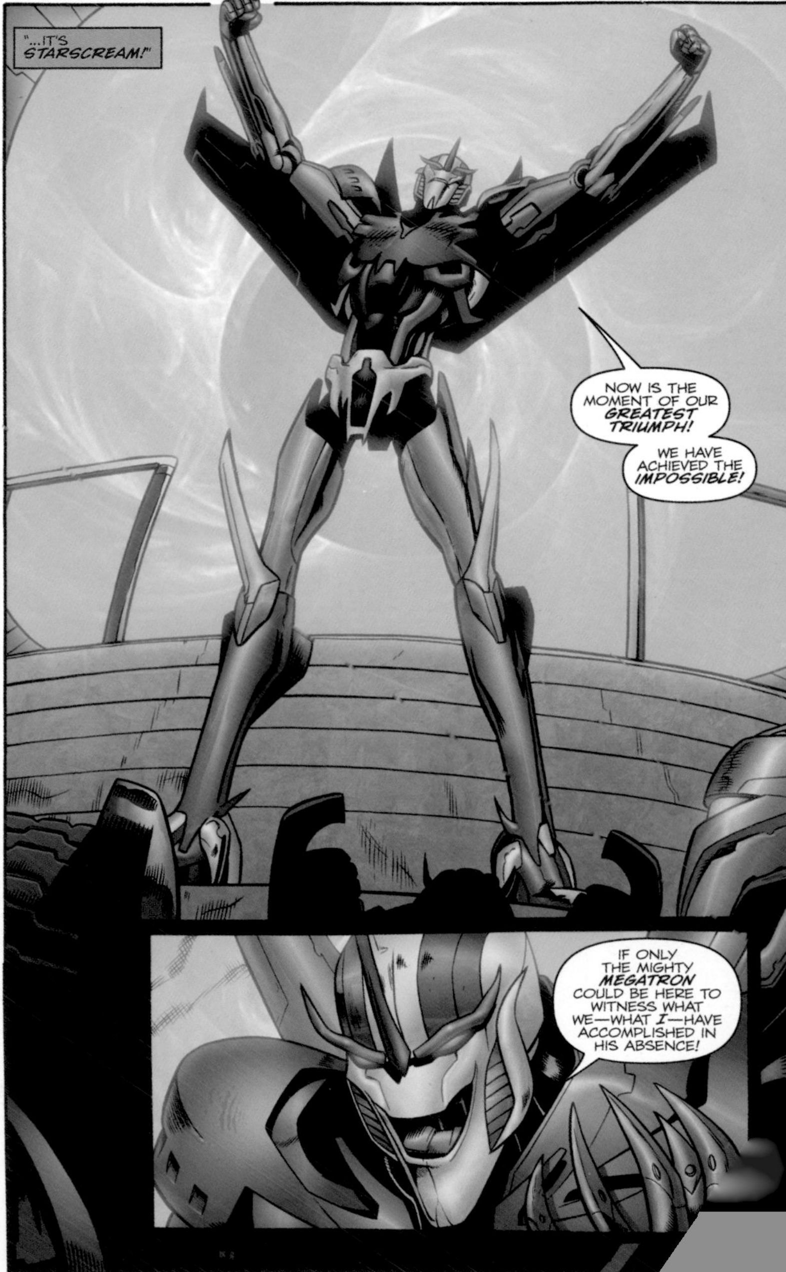
"...IT'S STARSCREAM!"
NOW IS THE MOMENT OF OUR GREATEST TRIUMPH!
WE HAVE ACHIEVED THE IMPOSSIBLE!
IF ONLY THE MIGHTY MEGATRON COULD BE HERE TO WITNESS WHAT WE—WHAT I—HAVE ACCOMPLISHED IN HIS ABSENCE!

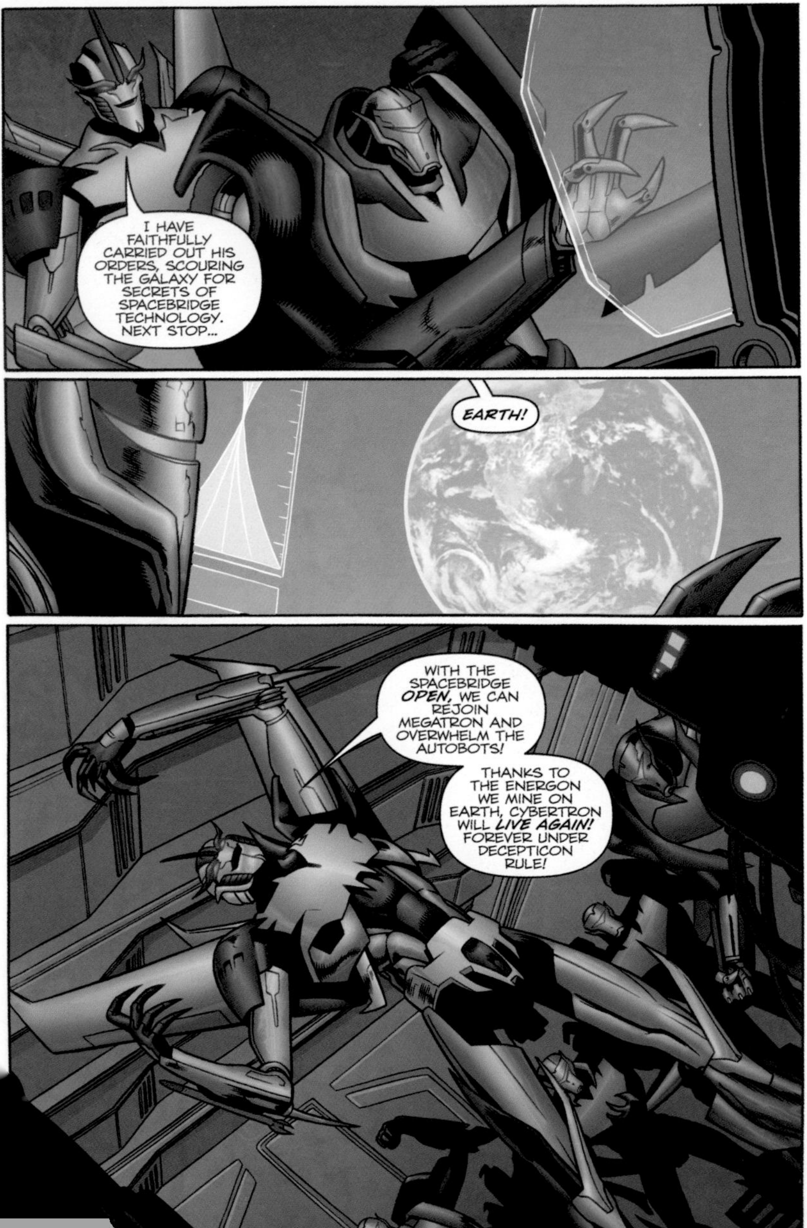
I HAVE FAITHFULLY CARRIED OUT HIS ORDERS, SCOURING THE GALAXY FOR SECRETS OF SPACEBRIDGE TECHNOLOGY. NEXT STOP...
EARTH!
WITH THE SPACEBRIDGE OPEN, WE CAN REJOIN MEGATRON AND OVERWHELM THE AUTOBOTS!
THANKS TO THE ENERGON WE MINE ON EARTH, CYBERTRON WILL LIVE AGAIN! FOREVER UNDER DECEPTICON RULE!

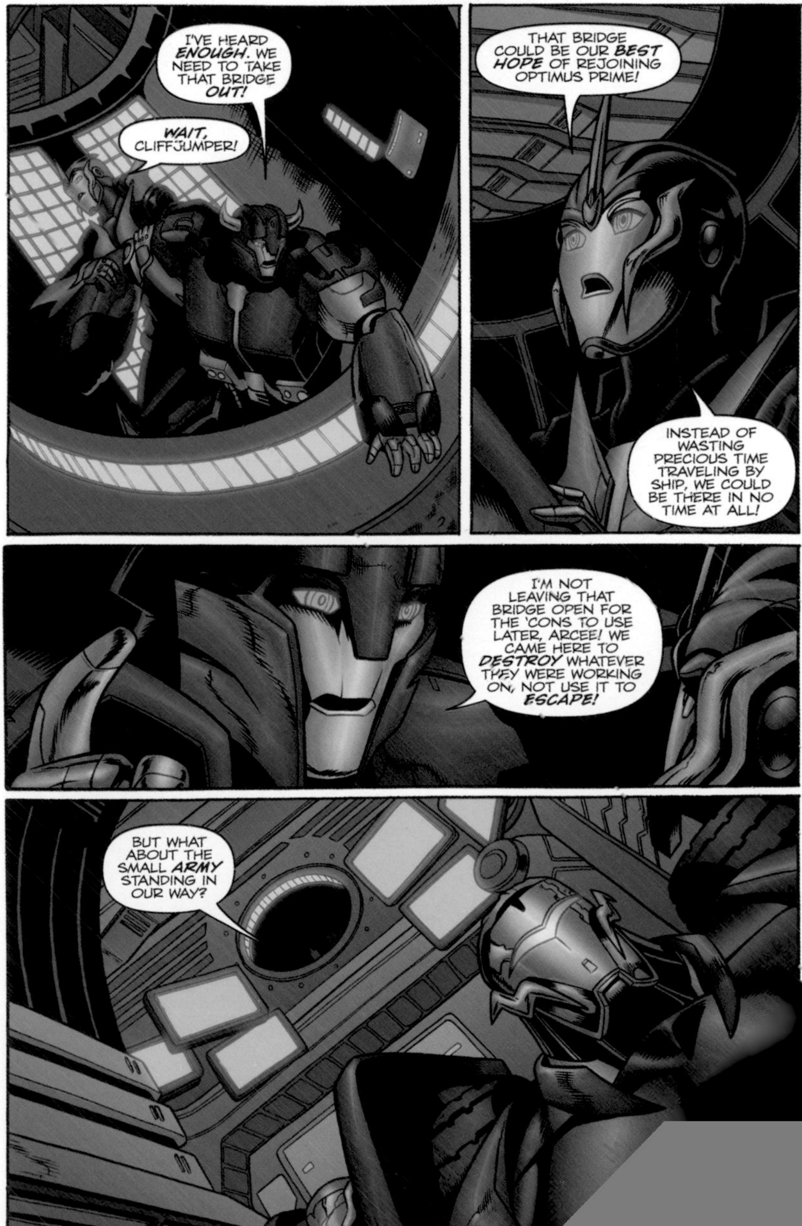

I'VE HEARD ENOUGH. WE NEED TO TAKE THAT BRIDGE OUT!
WAIT, CLIFFJUMPER!
THAT BRIDGE COULD BE OUR BEST HOPE OF REJOINING OPTIMUS PRIME!
INSTEAD OF WASTING PRECIOUS TIME TRAVELING BY SHIP, WE COULD BE THERE IN NO TIME AT ALL!
I'M NOT LEAVING THAT BRIDGE OPEN FOR THE 'CONS TO USE LATER, ARCEE! WE CAME HERE TO DESTROY WHATEVER THEY WERE WORKING ON, NOT USE IT TO ESCAPE!
BUT WHAT ABOUT THE SMALL ARMY STANDING IN OUR WAY?

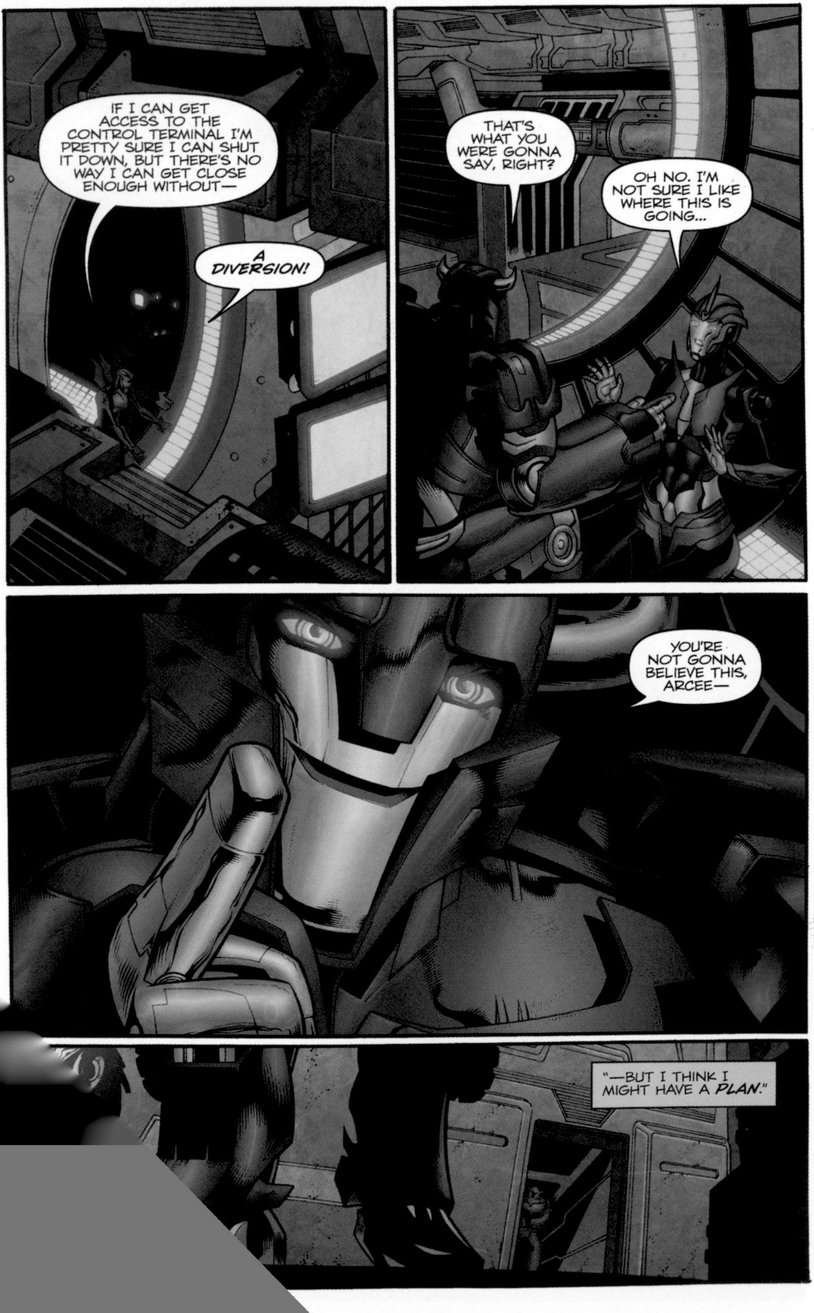
IF I CAN GET ACCESS TO THE CONTROL TERMINAL I'M PRETTY SURE I CAN SHUT IT DOWN, BUT THERE'S NO WAY I CAN GET CLOSE ENOUGH WITHOUT—
A *DIVERSION!*
THAT'S WHAT YOU WERE GONNA SAY, RIGHT?
OH NO. I'M NOT SURE I LIKE WHERE THIS IS GOING...
YOU'RE NOT GONNA BELIEVE THIS, ARCEE—
"—BUT I THINK I MIGHT HAVE A *PLAN*."

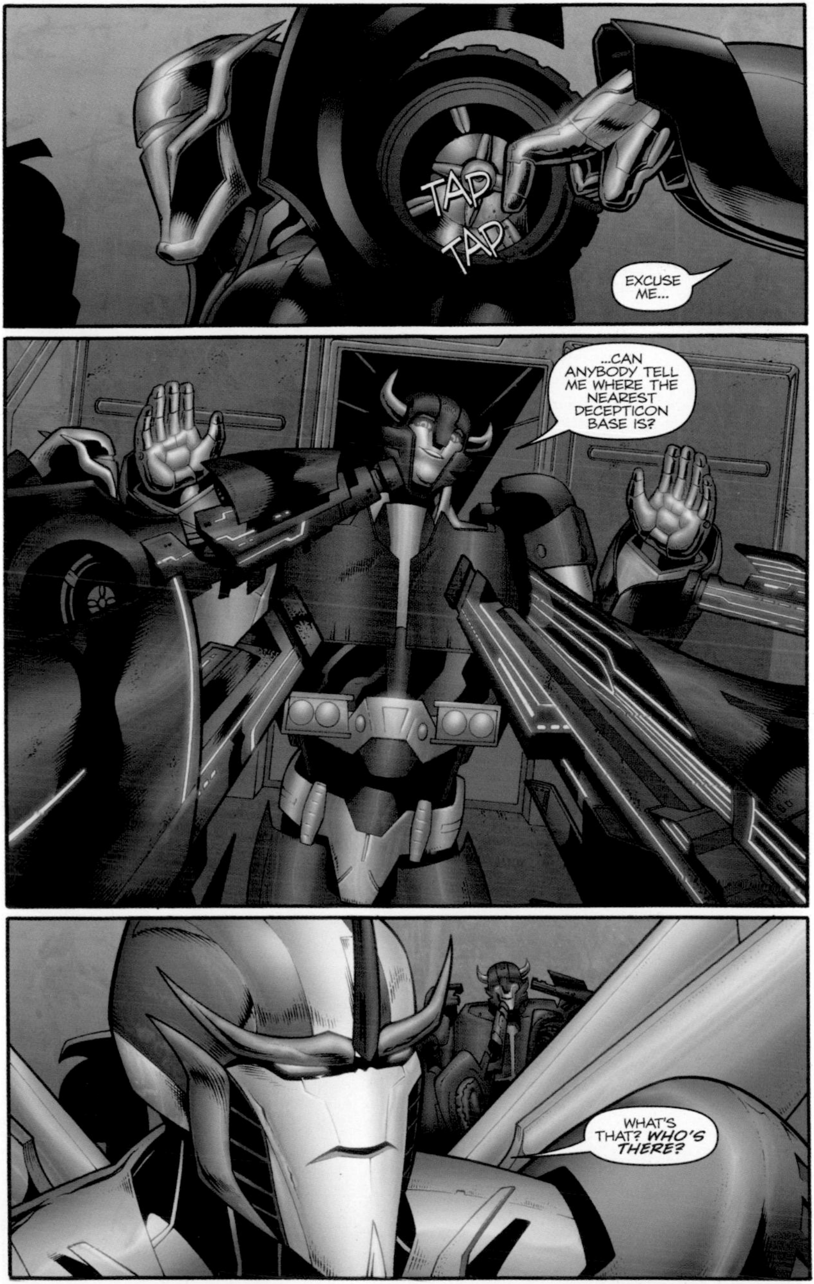
TAP
TAP
EXCUSE ME...
...CAN ANYBODY TELL ME WHERE THE NEAREST DECEPTICON BASE IS?
WHAT'S THAT? *WHO'S THERE?*

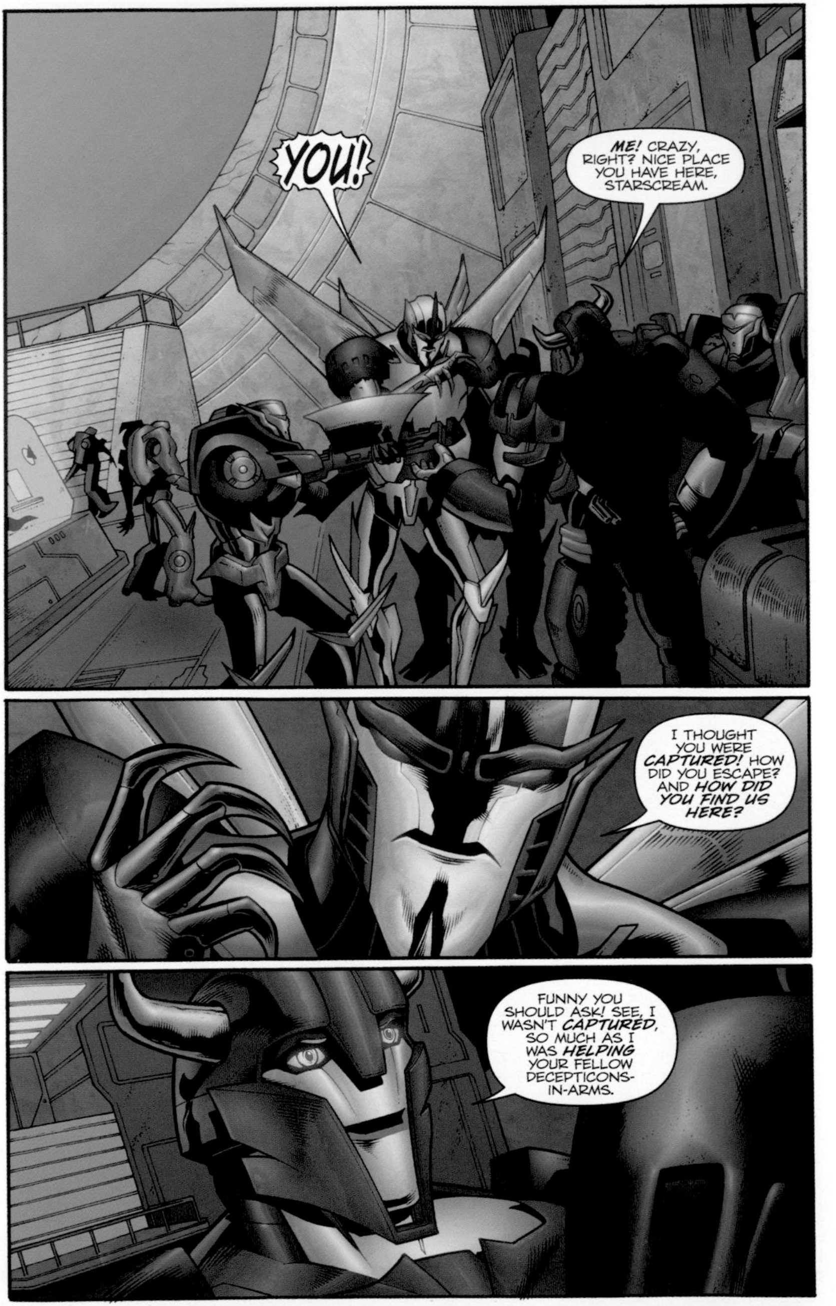
YOU!
ME! CRAZY, RIGHT? NICE PLACE YOU HAVE HERE, STARSCREAM.
I THOUGHT YOU WERE CAPTURED! HOW DID YOU ESCAPE? AND HOW DID YOU FIND US HERE?
FUNNY YOU SHOULD ASK! SEE, I WASN'T CAPTURED, SO MUCH AS I WAS HELPING YOUR FELLOW DECEPTICONS-IN-ARMS.

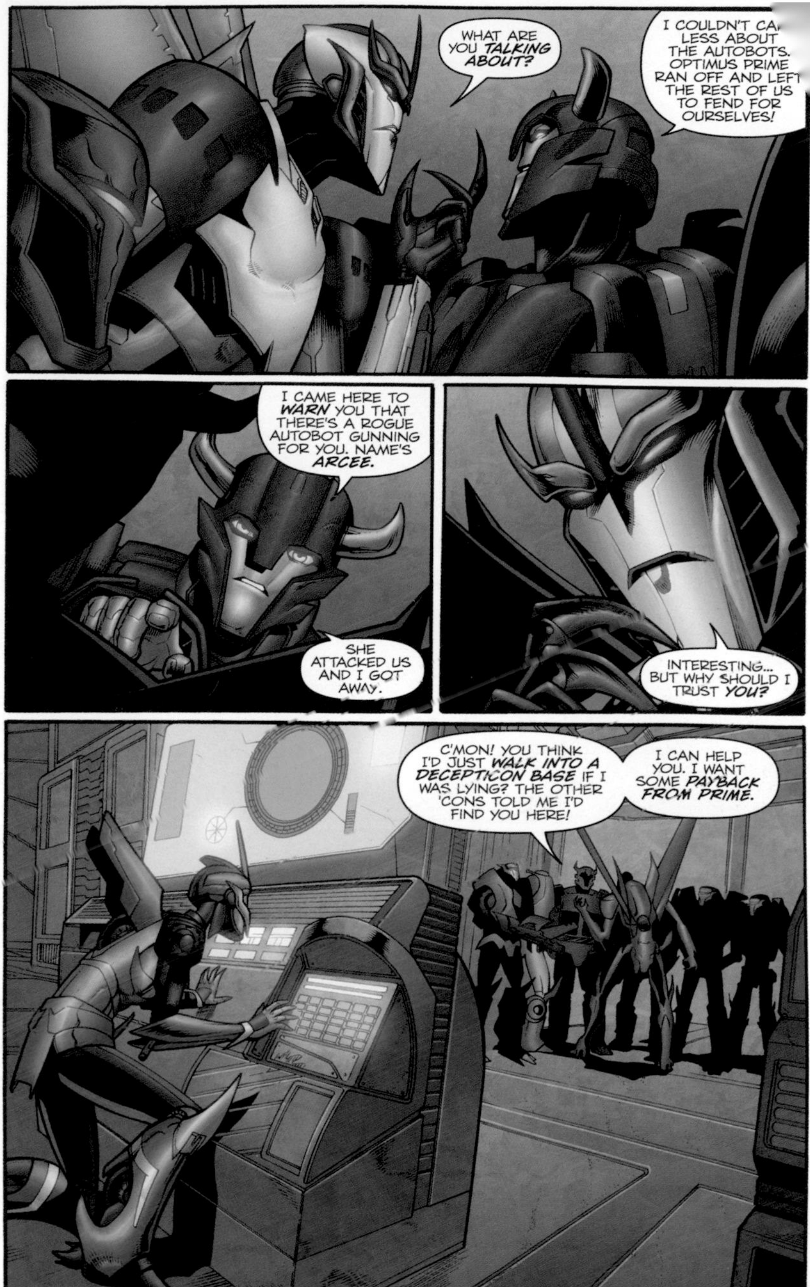
WHAT ARE YOU TALKING ABOUT?
I COULDN'T CA LESS ABOUT THE AUTOBOTS. OPTIMUS PRIME RAN OFF AND LEFT THE REST OF US TO FEND FOR OURSELVES!
I CAME HERE TO WARN YOU THAT THERE'S A ROGUE AUTOBOT GUNNING FOR YOU. NAME'S ARCEE.
SHE ATTACKED US AND I GOT AWAY.
INTERESTING... BUT WHY SHOULD I TRUST YOU?
C'MON! YOU THINK I'D JUST WALK INTO A DECEPTICON BASE IF I WAS LYING? THE OTHER 'CONS TOLD ME I'D FIND YOU HERE!
I CAN HELP YOU. I WANT SOME PAYBACK FROM PRIME.

KRRRAKKLE

EH? WHAT'S HAPPENING?

LOOKS LIKE SOMETHING'S WRONG WITH YOUR SPACEBRIDGE!

YOU! STOP! WHAT ARE YOU DOING!?

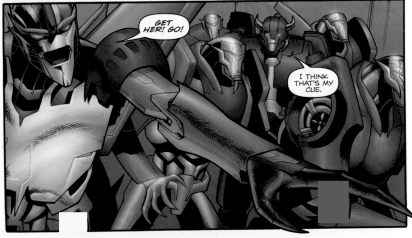

GET HER! GO!

I THINK THAT'S MY CUE.

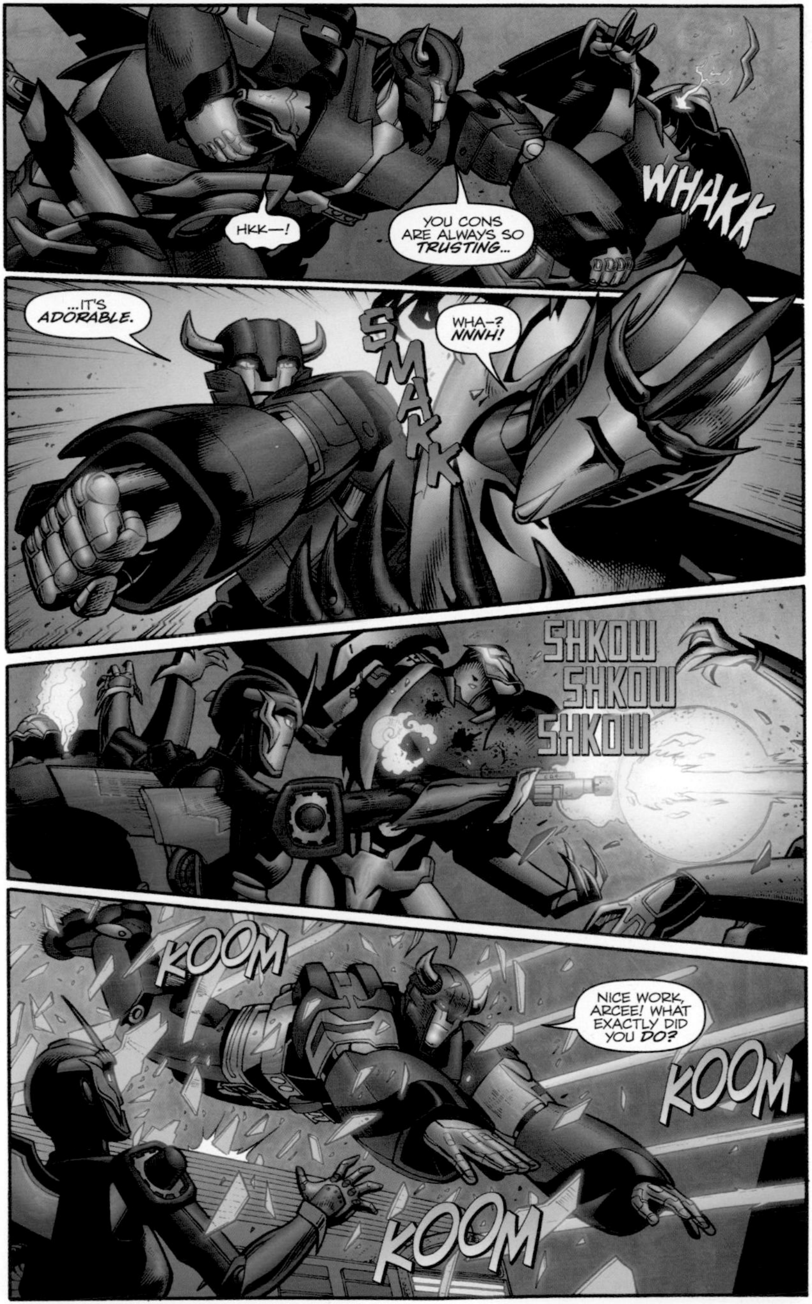
HKK—!
YOU CONS ARE ALWAYS SO TRUSTING...
WHAKK
...IT'S ADORABLE.
SMAKK
WHA—? NNNH!
SHKOW
SHKOW
SHKOW
KOOM
NICE WORK, ARCEE! WHAT EXACTLY DID YOU DO?
KOOM
KOOM

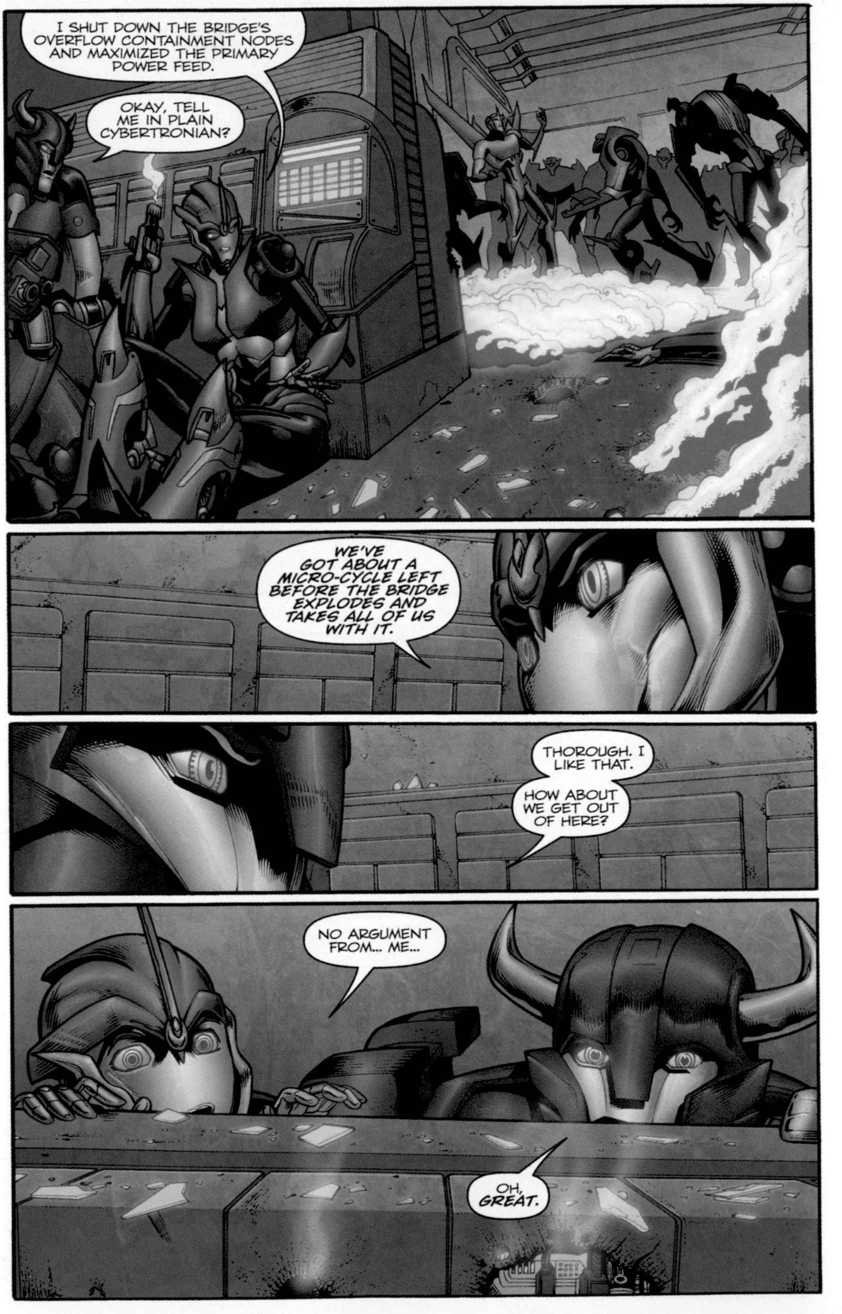

I SHUT DOWN THE BRIDGE'S OVERFLOW CONTAINMENT NODES AND MAXIMIZED THE PRIMARY POWER FEED.
OKAY, TELL ME IN PLAIN CYBERTRONIAN?
WE'VE GOT ABOUT A MICRO-CYCLE LEFT BEFORE THE BRIDGE EXPLODES AND TAKES ALL OF US WITH IT.
THOROUGH. I LIKE THAT.
HOW ABOUT WE GET OUT OF HERE?
NO ARGUMENT FROM... ME...
OH, GREAT.

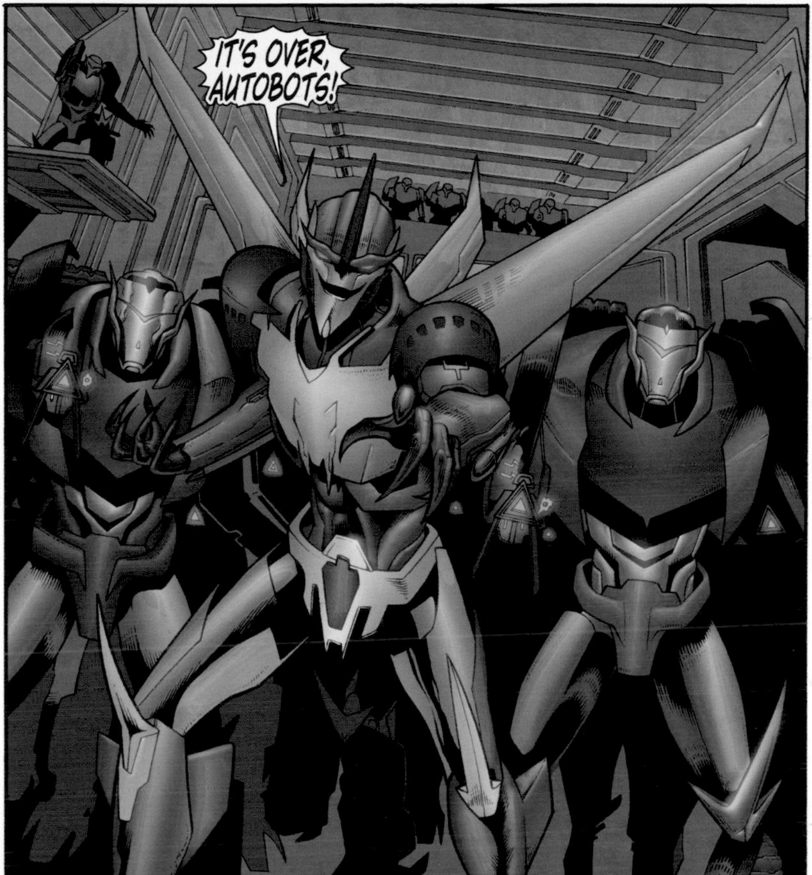
IT'S OVER, AUTOBOTS!

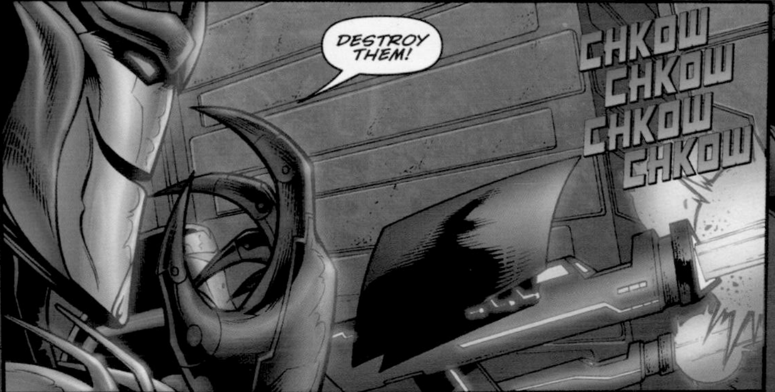
DESTROY THEM!
CHKOW CHKOW CHKOW CHKOW

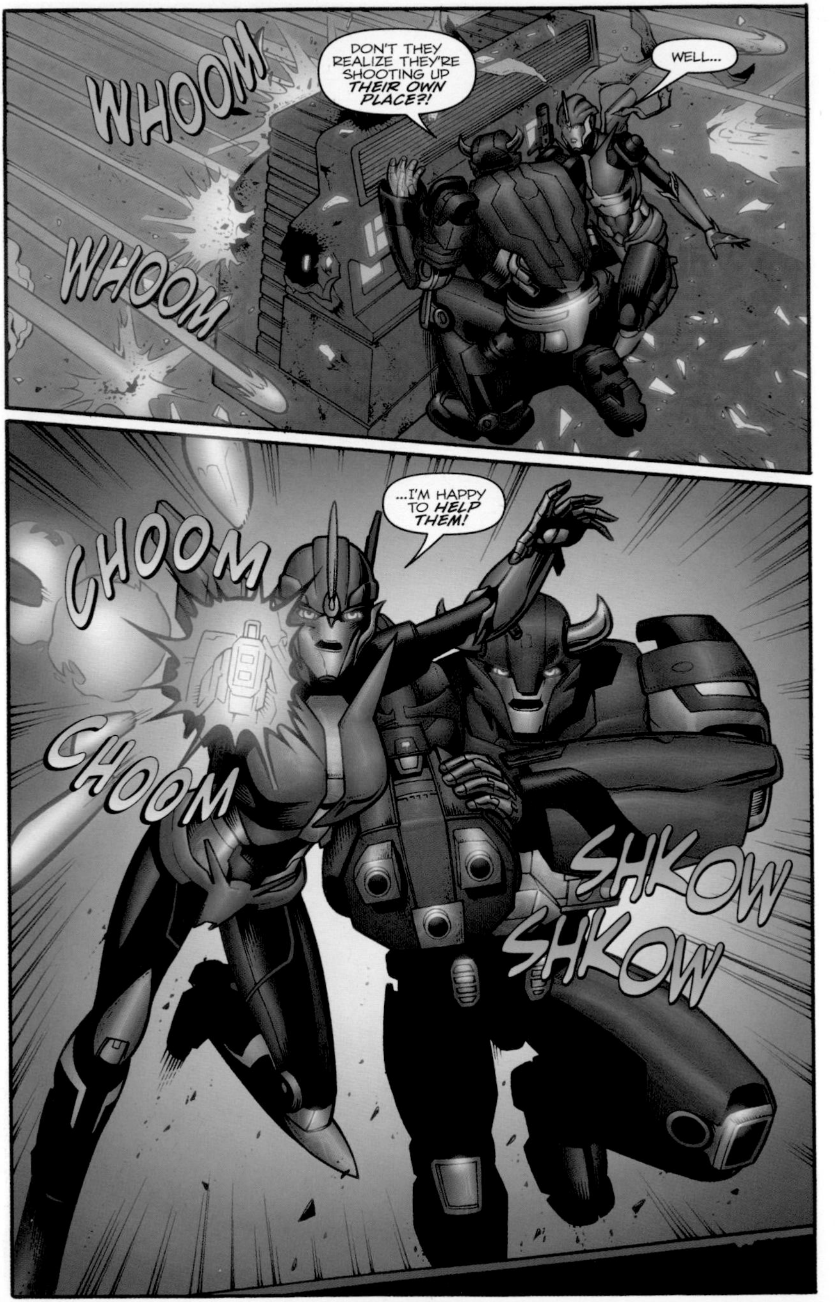
WHOOM
WHOOM
DON'T THEY REALIZE THEY'RE SHOOTING UP *THEIR OWN PLACE?!*
WELL...
...I'M HAPPY TO *HELP THEM!*
CHOOM
CHOOM
SHKOW
SHKOW

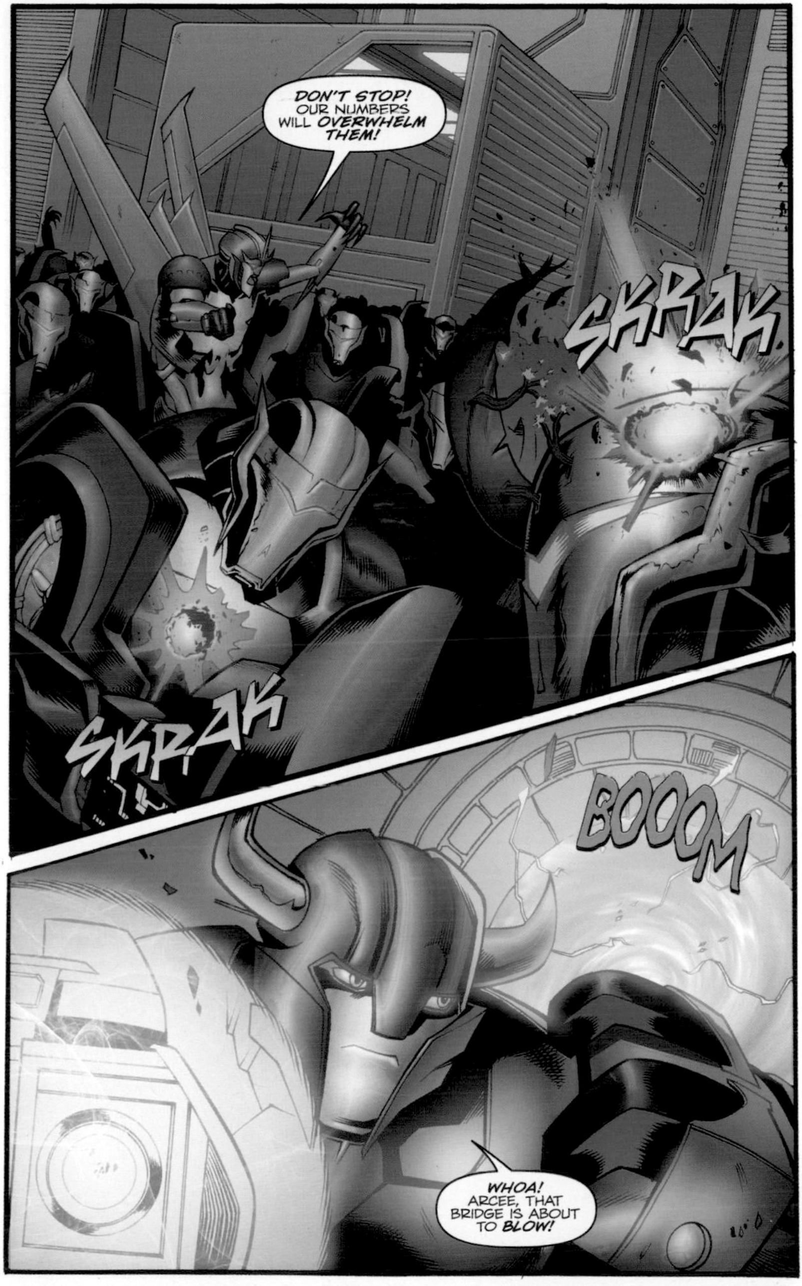
DON'T STOP! OUR NUMBERS WILL OVERWHELM THEM!
SKRAK
SKRAK
BOOOM
WHOA! ARCEE, THAT BRIDGE IS ABOUT TO BLOW!

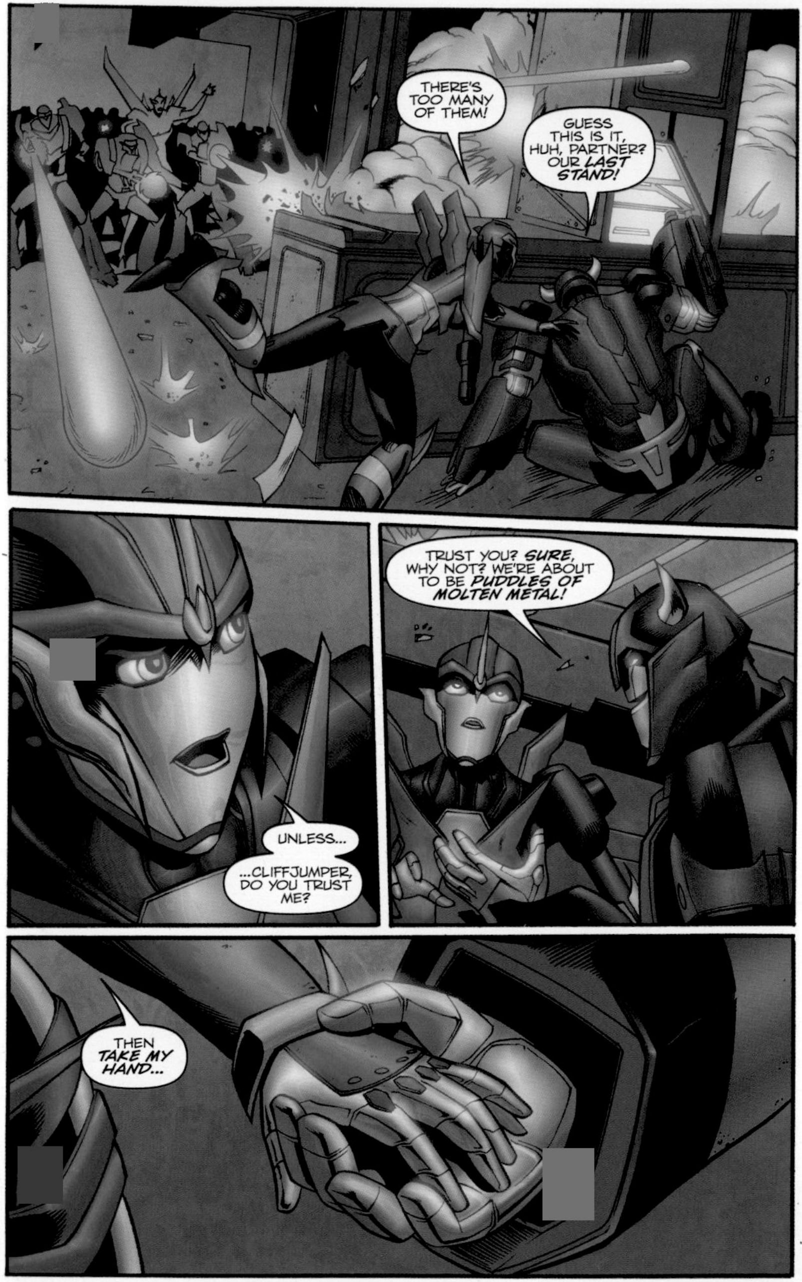
THERE'S TOO MANY OF THEM!
GUESS THIS IS IT, HUH, PARTNER? OUR LAST STAND!
UNLESS...
...CLIFFJUMPER, DO YOU TRUST ME?
TRUST YOU? SURE, WHY NOT? WE'RE ABOUT TO BE PUDDLES OF MOLTEN METAL!
THEN TAKE MY HAND...

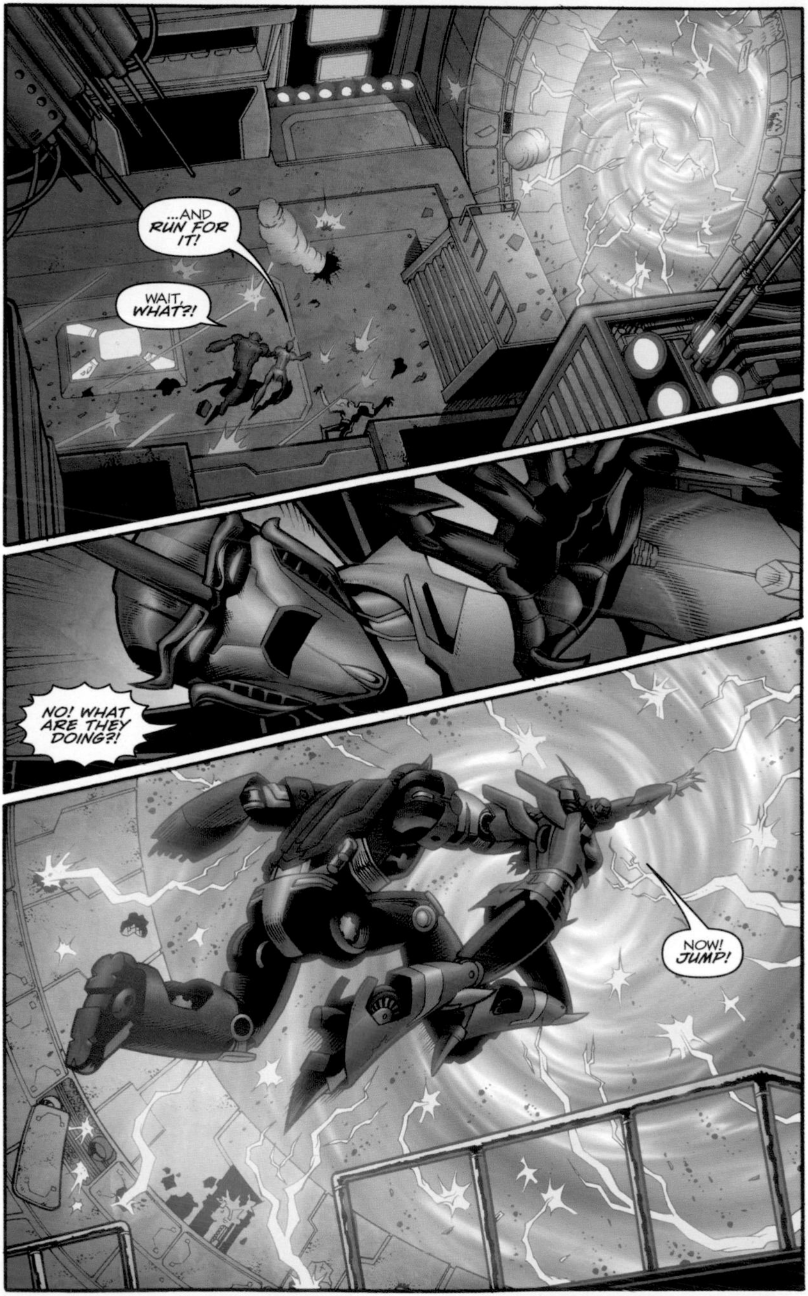
...AND RUN FOR IT!
WAIT, WHAT?!
NO! WHAT ARE THEY DOING?!
NOW! JUMP!

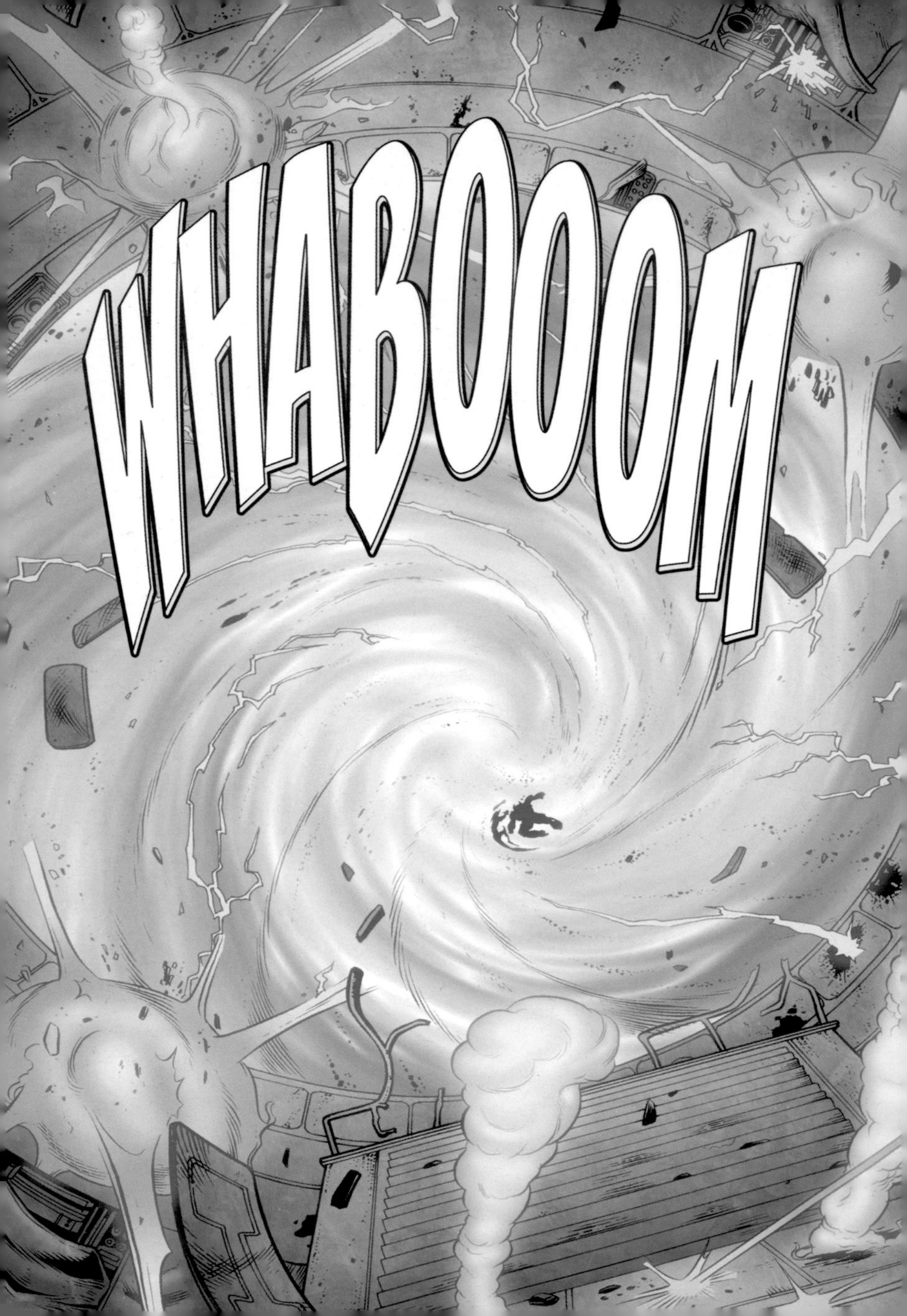
WHABOOOM

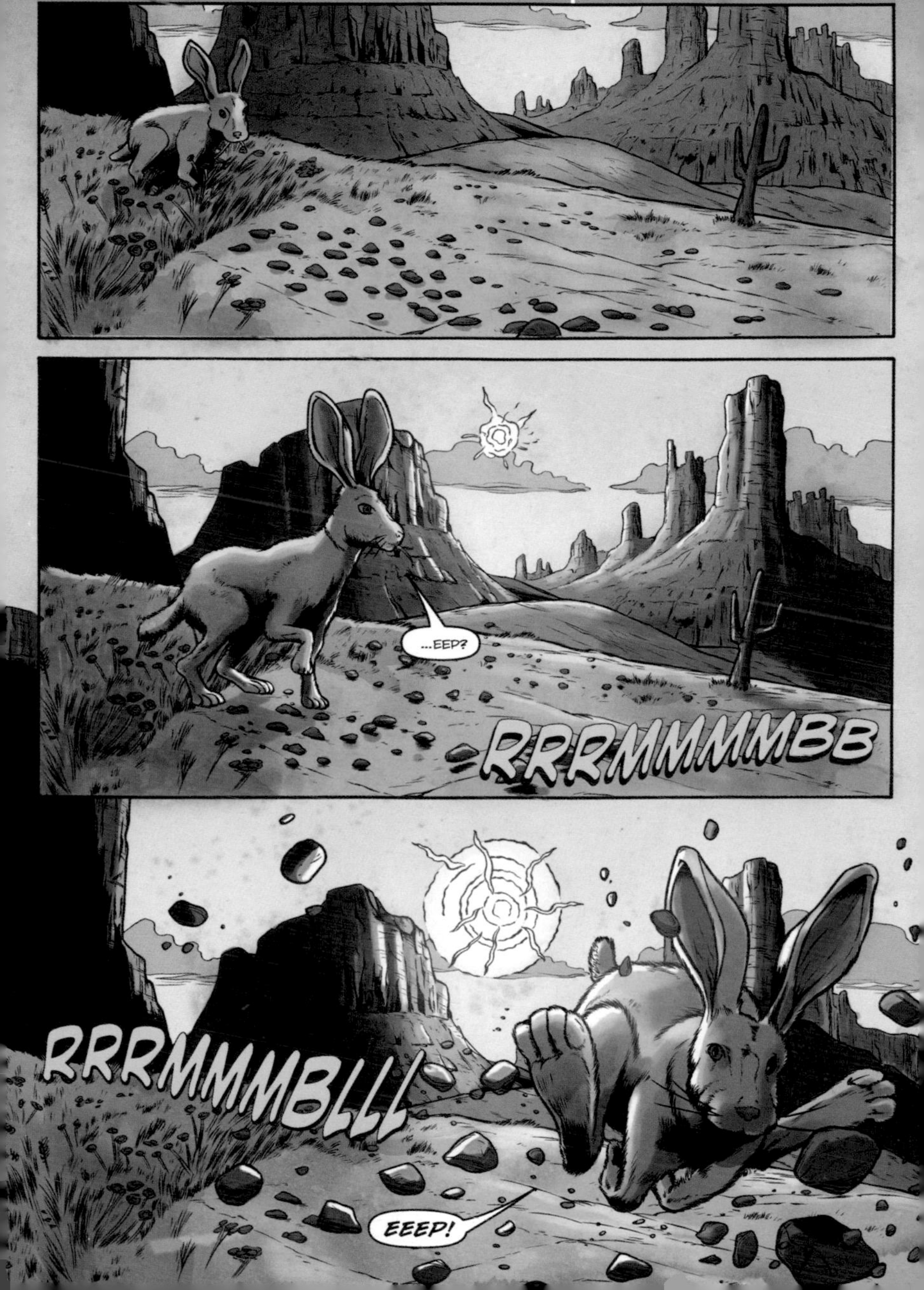
...EEP?
RRRMMMMMBB
RRRMMMMBLLL
EEEP!

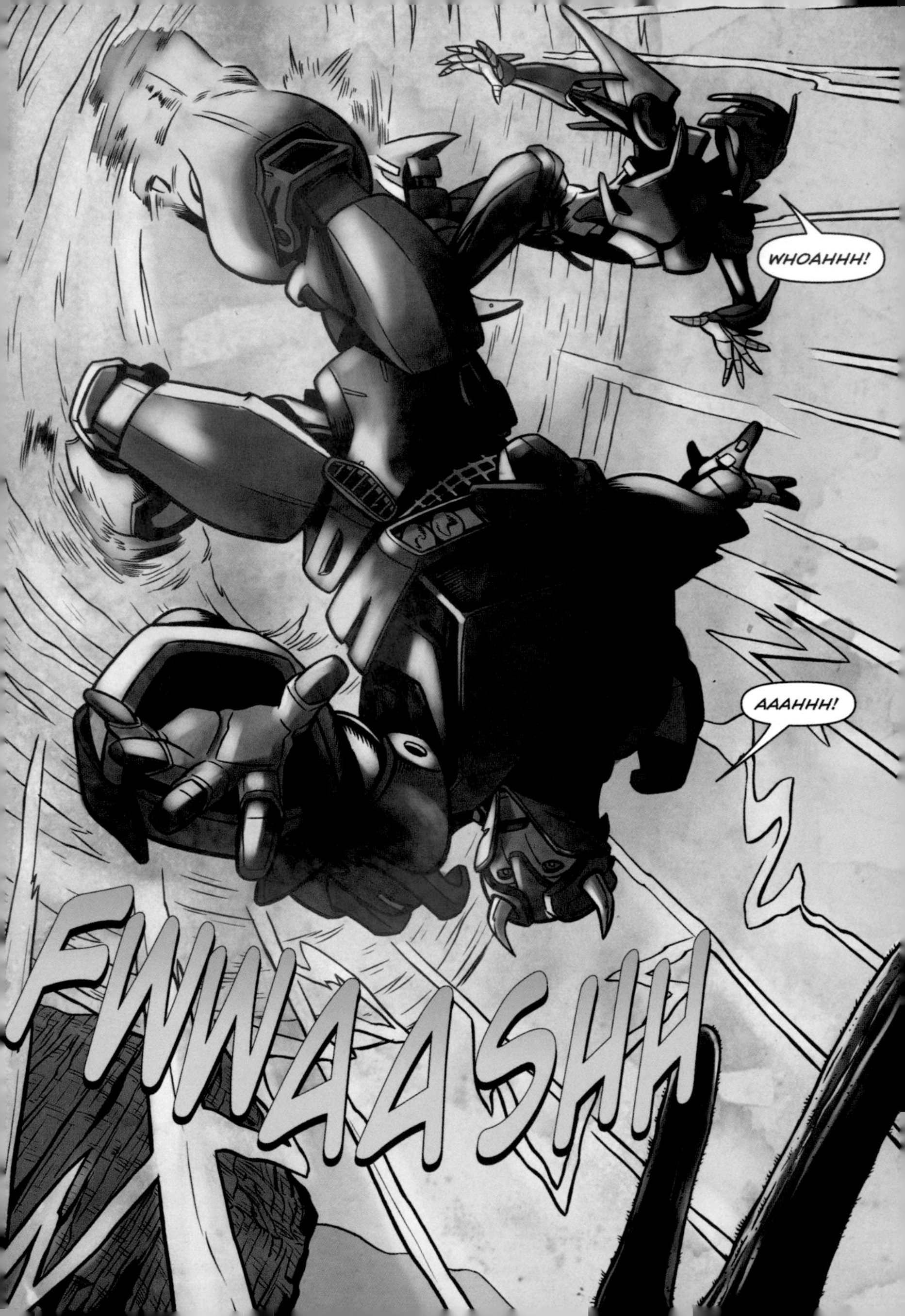
WHOAHHH!
AAAHHH!
FWWAASHH

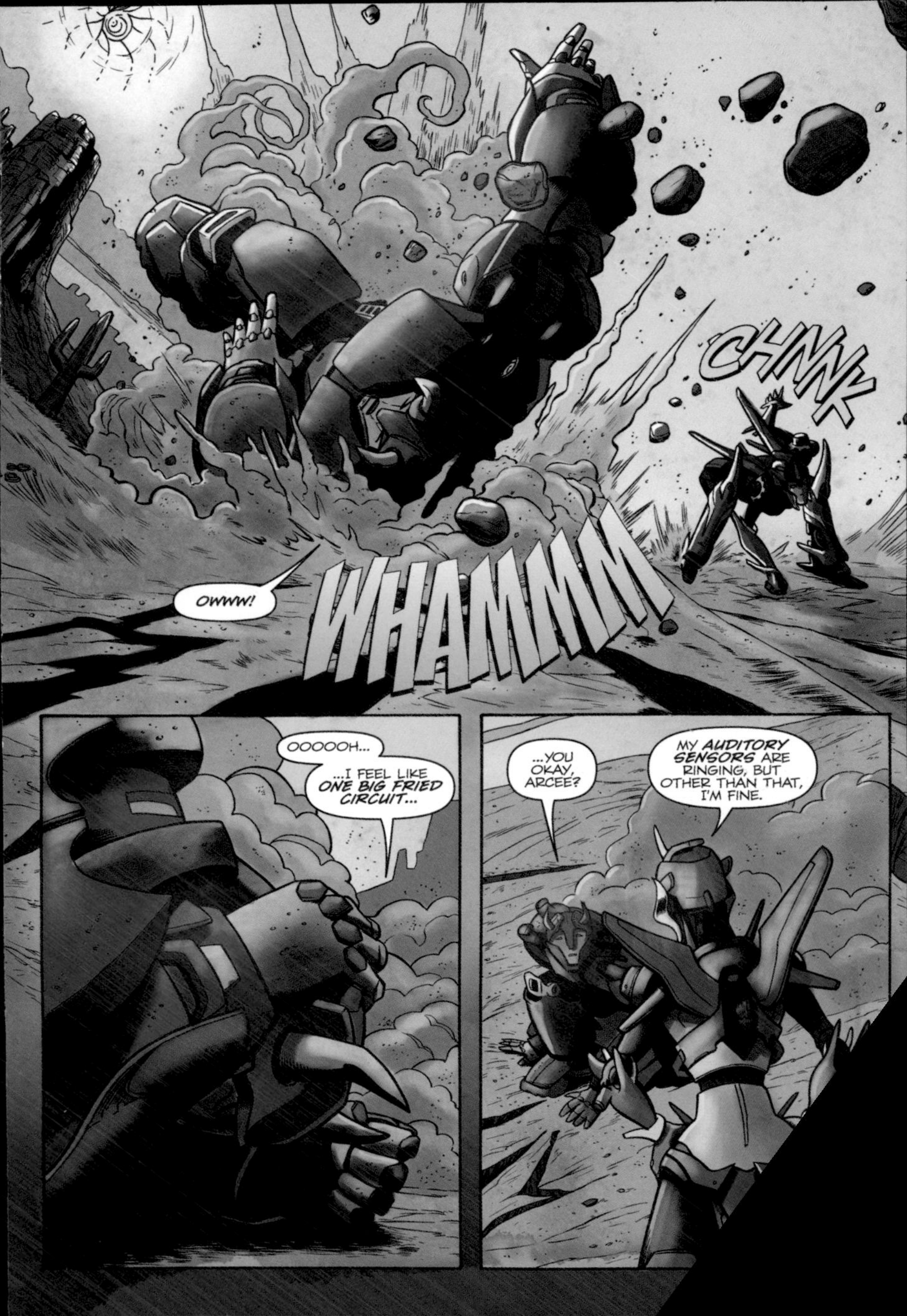
CHNNK
OWWW!
WHAMMM!
OOOOOH...
...I FEEL LIKE ONE BIG FRIED CIRCUIT...
...YOU OKAY, ARCEE?
MY AUDITORY SENSORS ARE RINGING, BUT OTHER THAN THAT, I'M FINE.

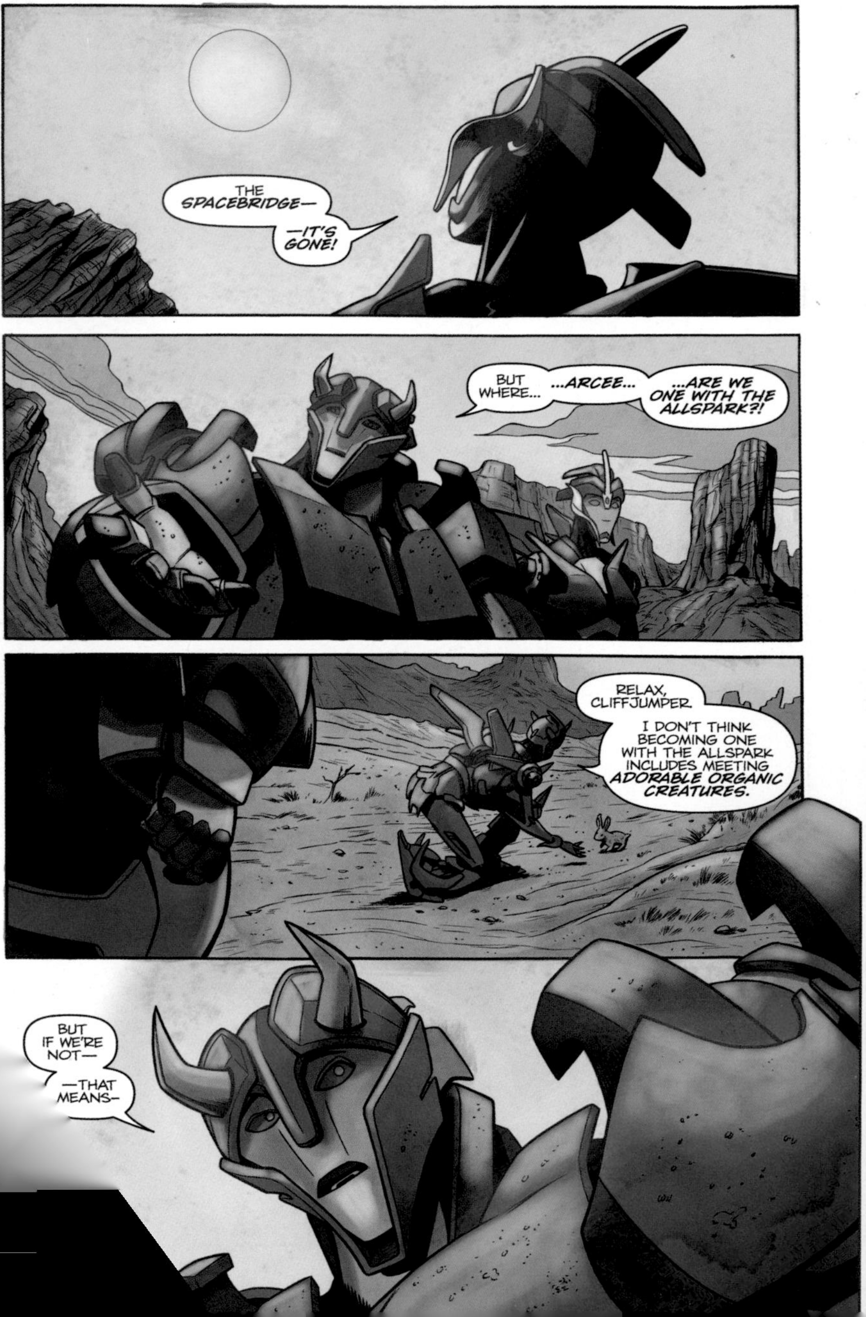
THE SPACEBRIDGE—
—IT'S GONE!
BUT WHERE...
...ARCEE...
...ARE WE ONE WITH THE ALLSPARK?!
RELAX, CLIFFJUMPER.
I DON'T THINK BECOMING ONE WITH THE ALLSPARK INCLUDES MEETING ***ADORABLE ORGANIC CREATURES.***
BUT IF WE'RE NOT—
—THAT MEANS—

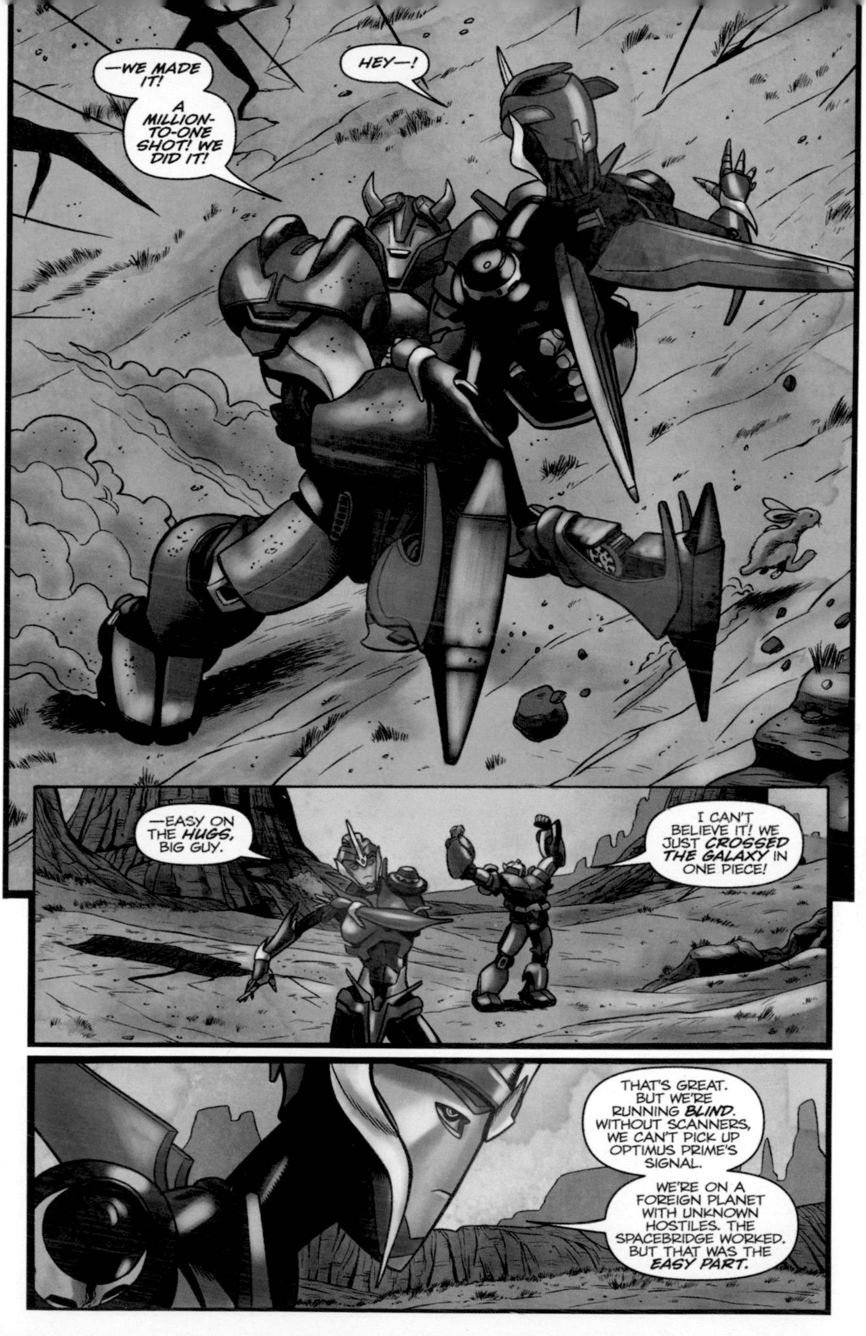

—WE MADE IT!
A MILLION-TO-ONE SHOT! WE DID IT!
HEY—!
—EASY ON THE HUGS, BIG GUY.
I CAN'T BELIEVE IT! WE JUST CROSSED THE GALAXY IN ONE PIECE!
THAT'S GREAT. BUT WE'RE RUNNING BLIND. WITHOUT SCANNERS, WE CAN'T PICK UP OPTIMUS PRIME'S SIGNAL.
WE'RE ON A FOREIGN PLANET WITH UNKNOWN HOSTILES. THE SPACEBRIDGE WORKED. BUT THAT WAS THE EASY PART.

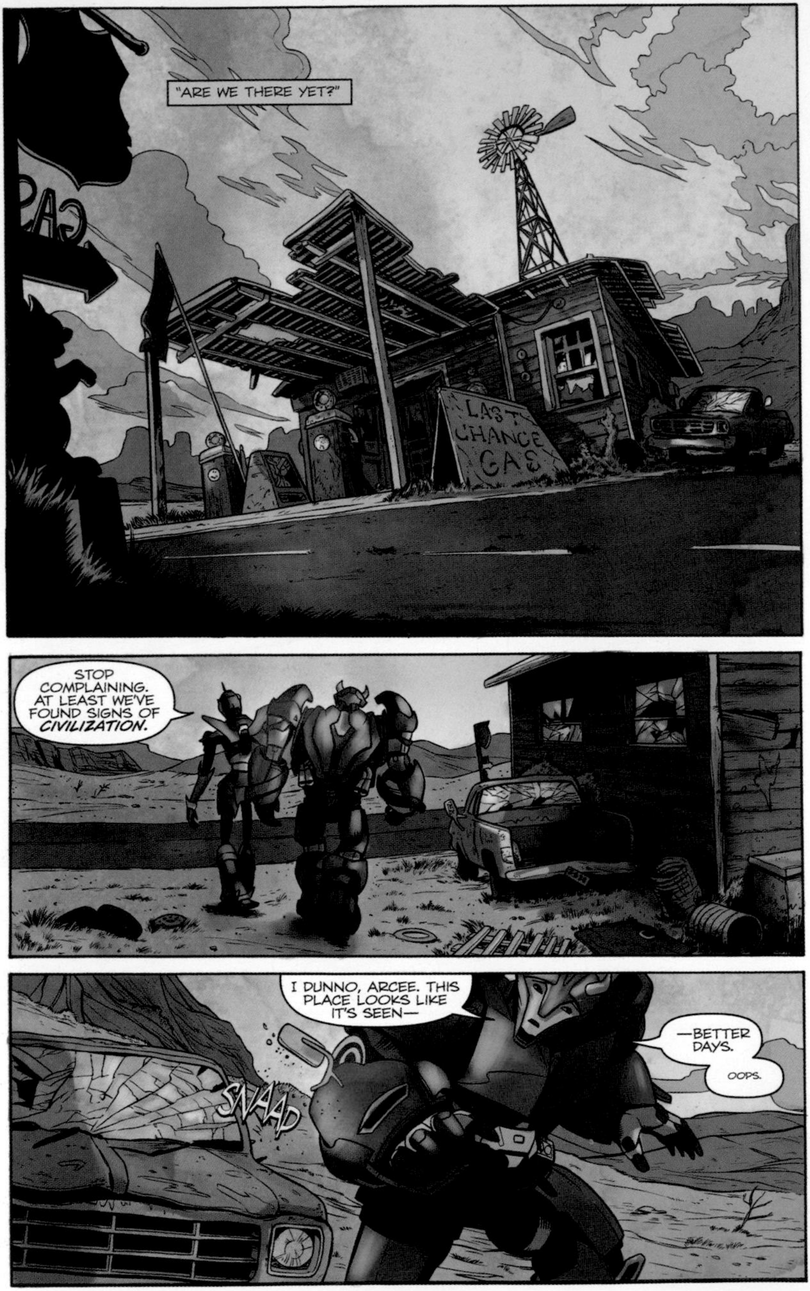
"ARE WE THERE YET?"
GAS
LAST CHANCE GAS
STOP COMPLAINING. AT LEAST WE'VE FOUND SIGNS OF *CIVILIZATION.*
I DUNNO, ARCEE. THIS PLACE LOOKS LIKE IT'S SEEN—
SNAAP
—BETTER DAYS.
OOPS.

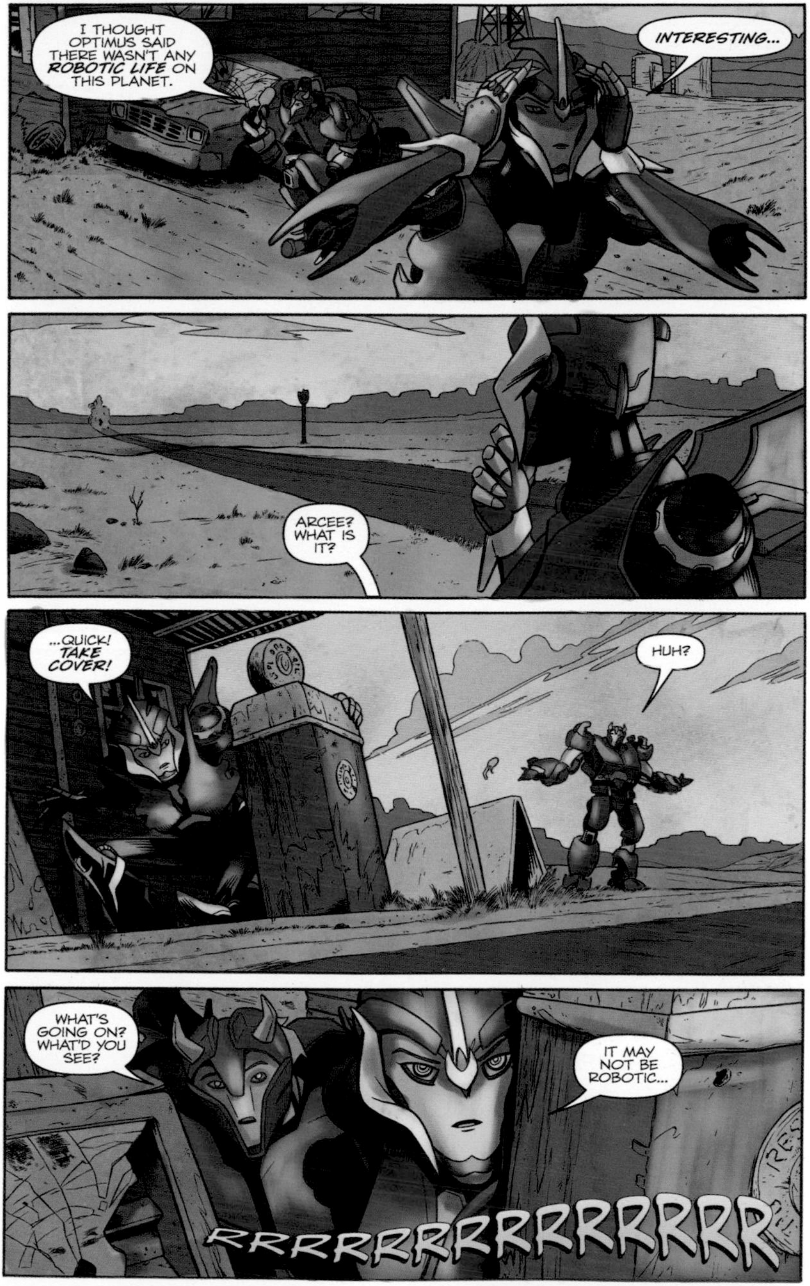
I THOUGHT OPTIMUS SAID THERE WASN'T ANY ROBOTIC LIFE ON THIS PLANET.
INTERESTING...
ARCEE? WHAT IS IT?
...QUICK! TAKE COVER!
HUH?
WHAT'S GOING ON? WHAT'D YOU SEE?
IT MAY NOT BE ROBOTIC...
RRRRRRRRRRRRRRRR

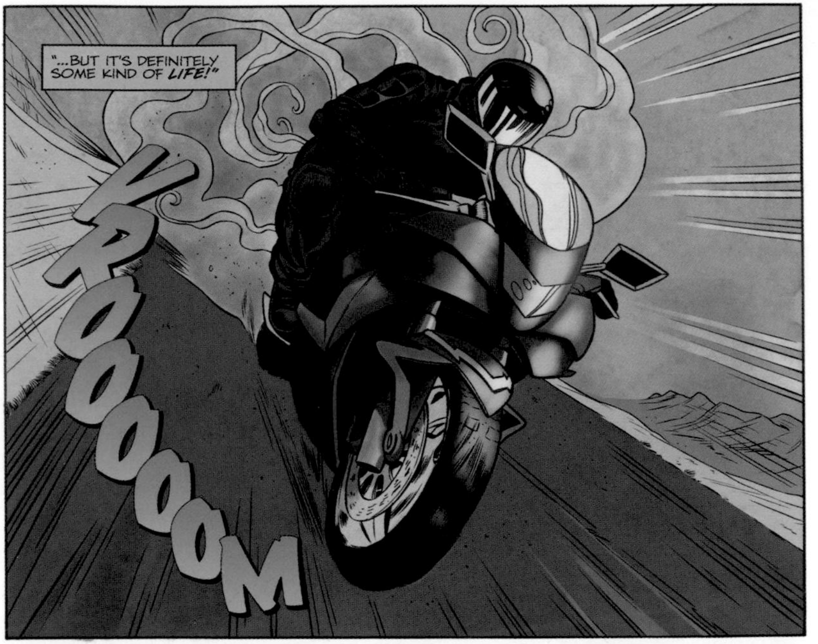
"...BUT IT'S DEFINITELY SOME KIND OF LIFE!"
VRROOOOOOM

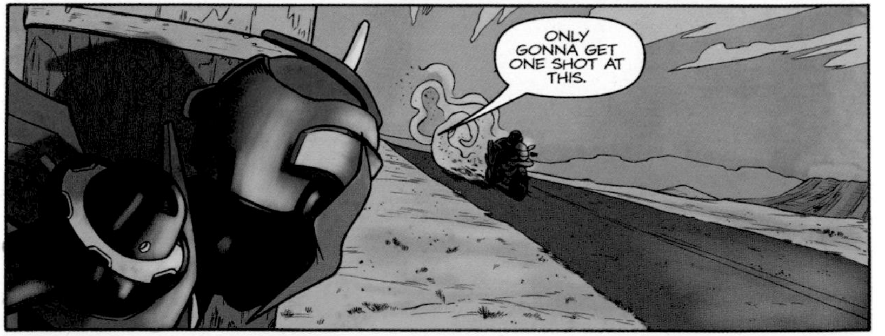
ONLY GONNA GET ONE SHOT AT THIS.

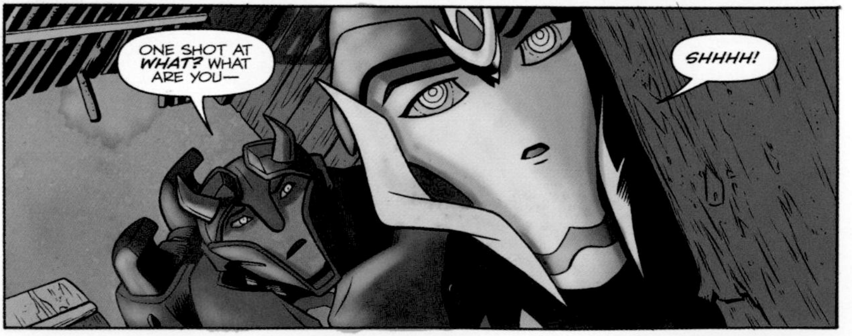
ONE SHOT AT WHAT? WHAT ARE YOU—
SHHHH!

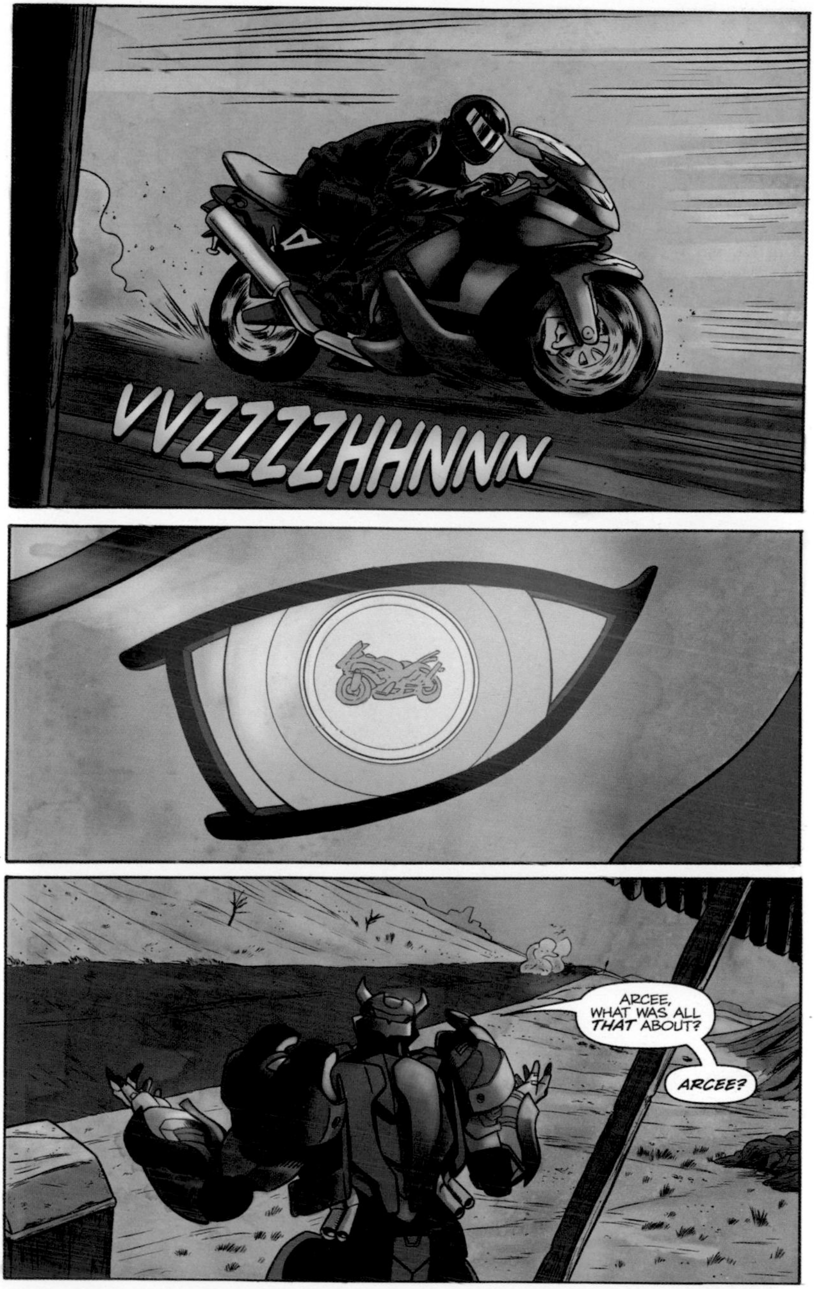
VVZZZZZHHNNN
ARCEE, WHAT WAS ALL THAT ABOUT?
ARCEE?

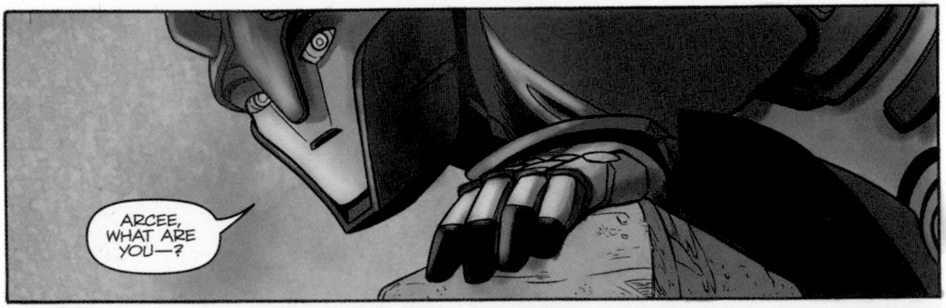
ARCEE, WHAT ARE YOU—?
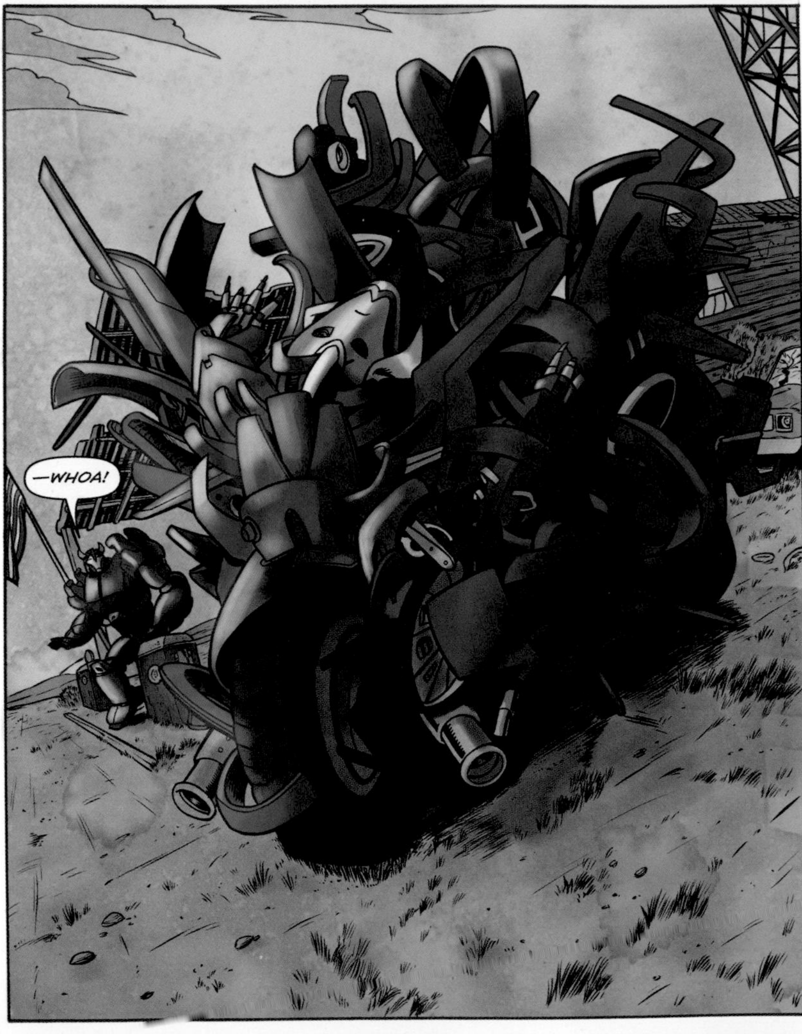
—WHOA!

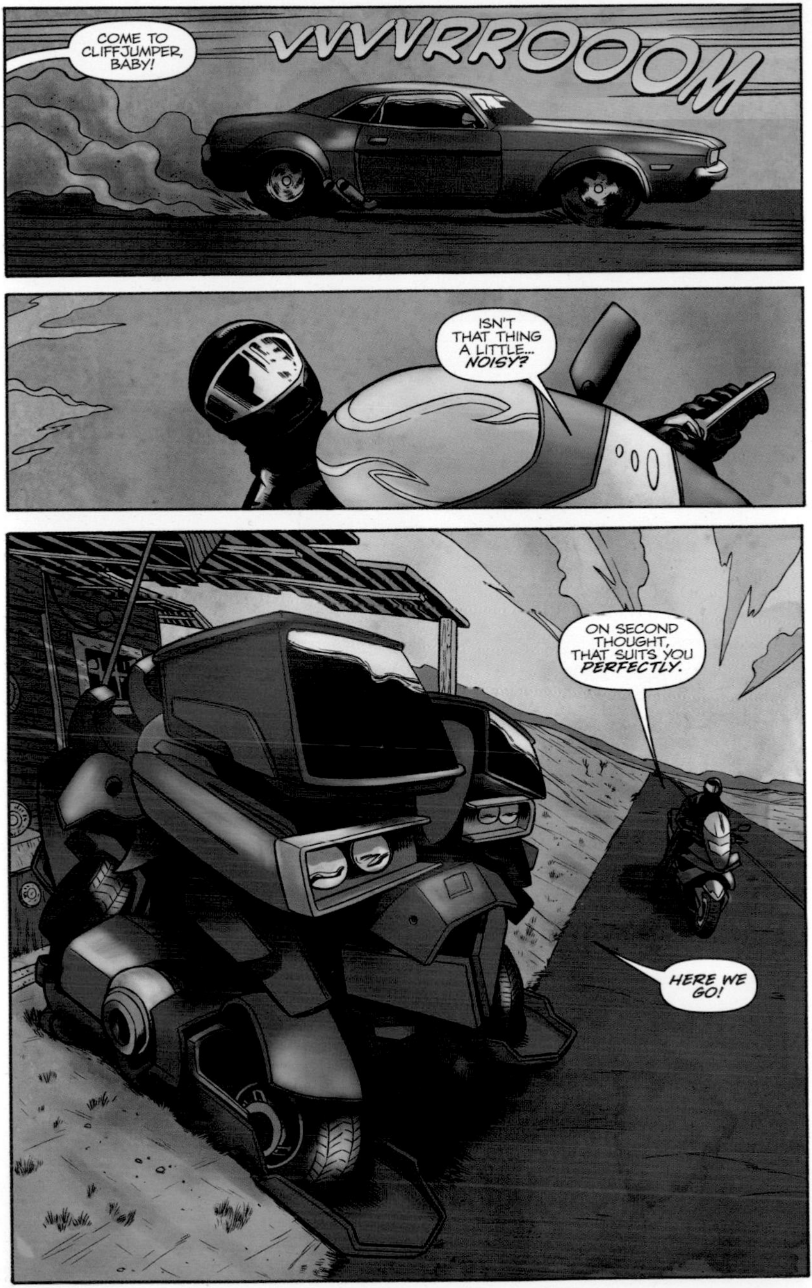

COME TO CLIFFJUMPER, BABY!
VVVVRROOOOM
ISN'T THAT THING A LITTLE... NOISY?
ON SECOND THOUGHT, THAT SUITS YOU PERFECTLY.
HERE WE GO!

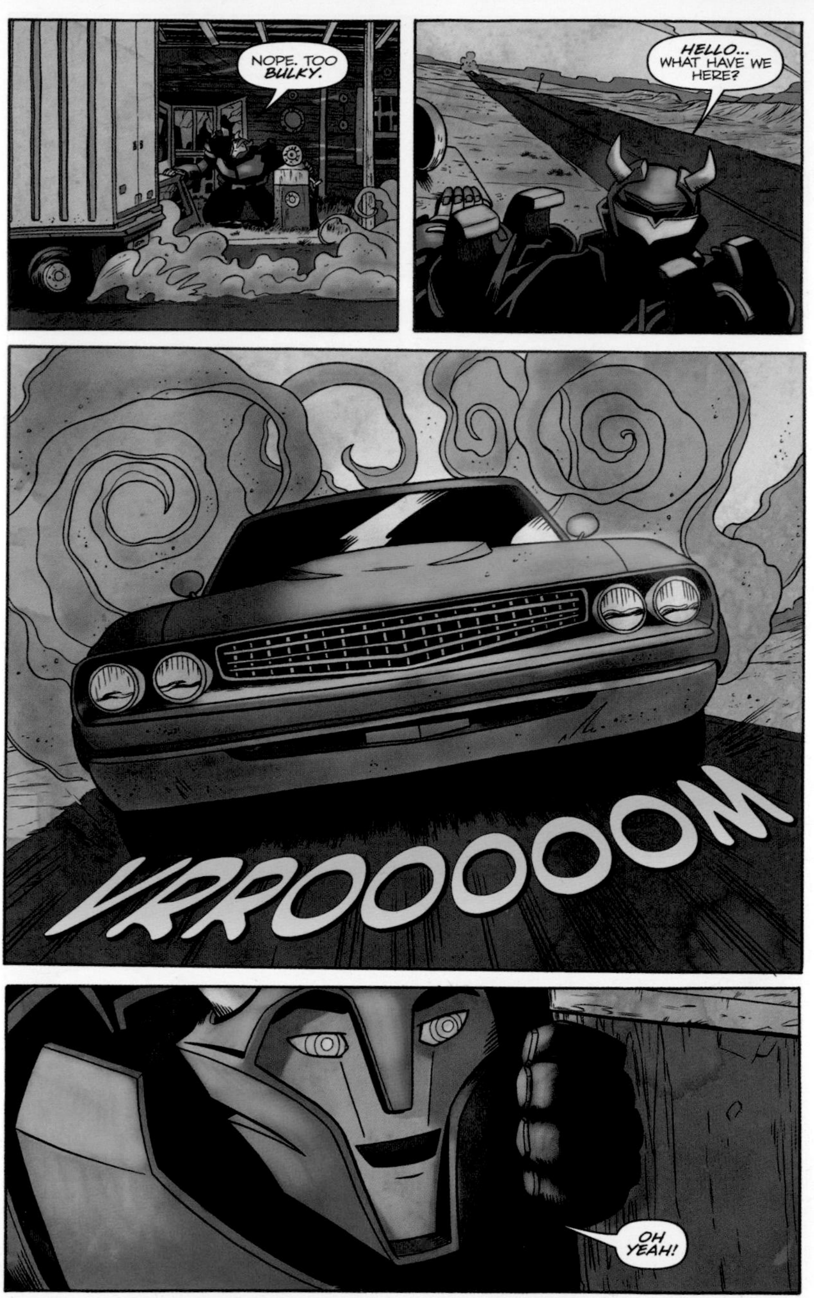
NOPE. TOO *BULKY.*
HELLO... WHAT HAVE WE HERE?
VRROOOOOOM
OH YEAH!

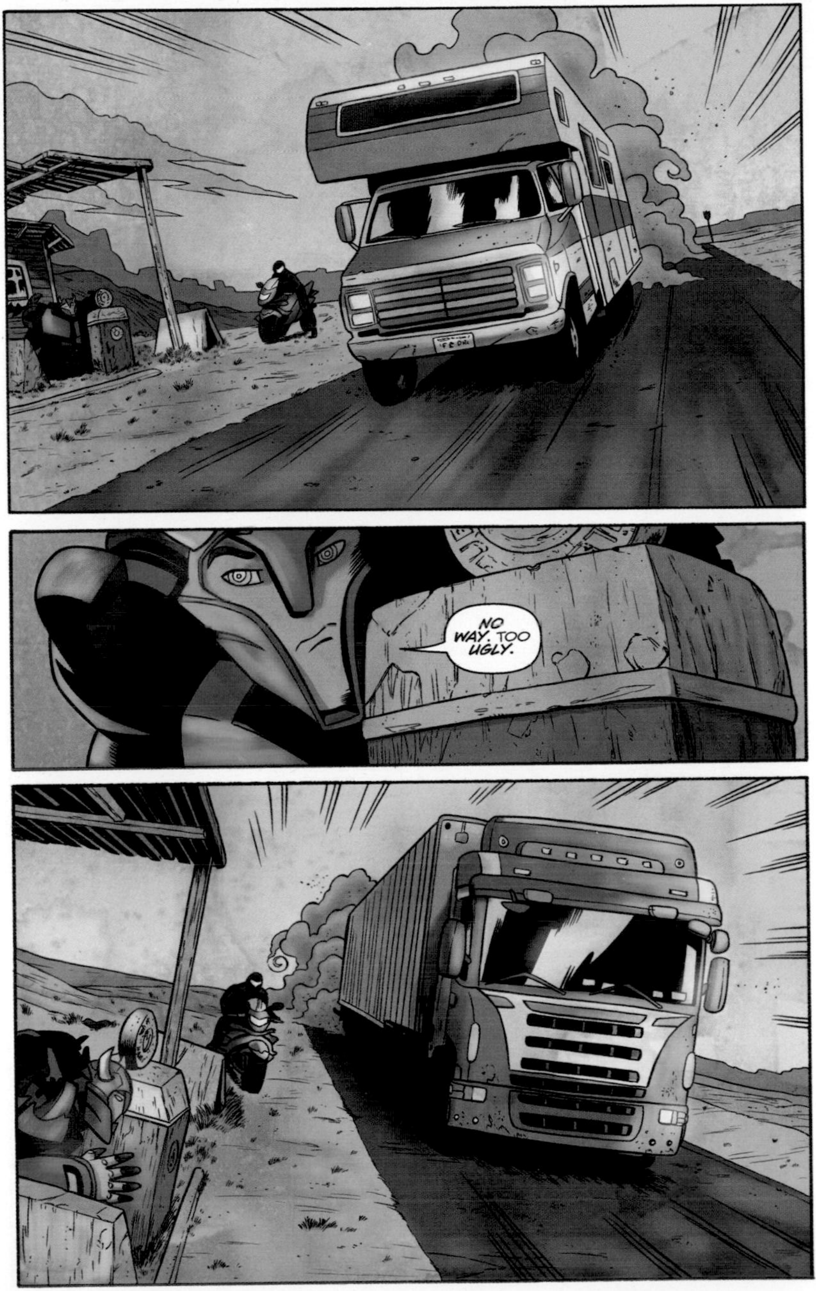
NO WAY. TOO UGLY.

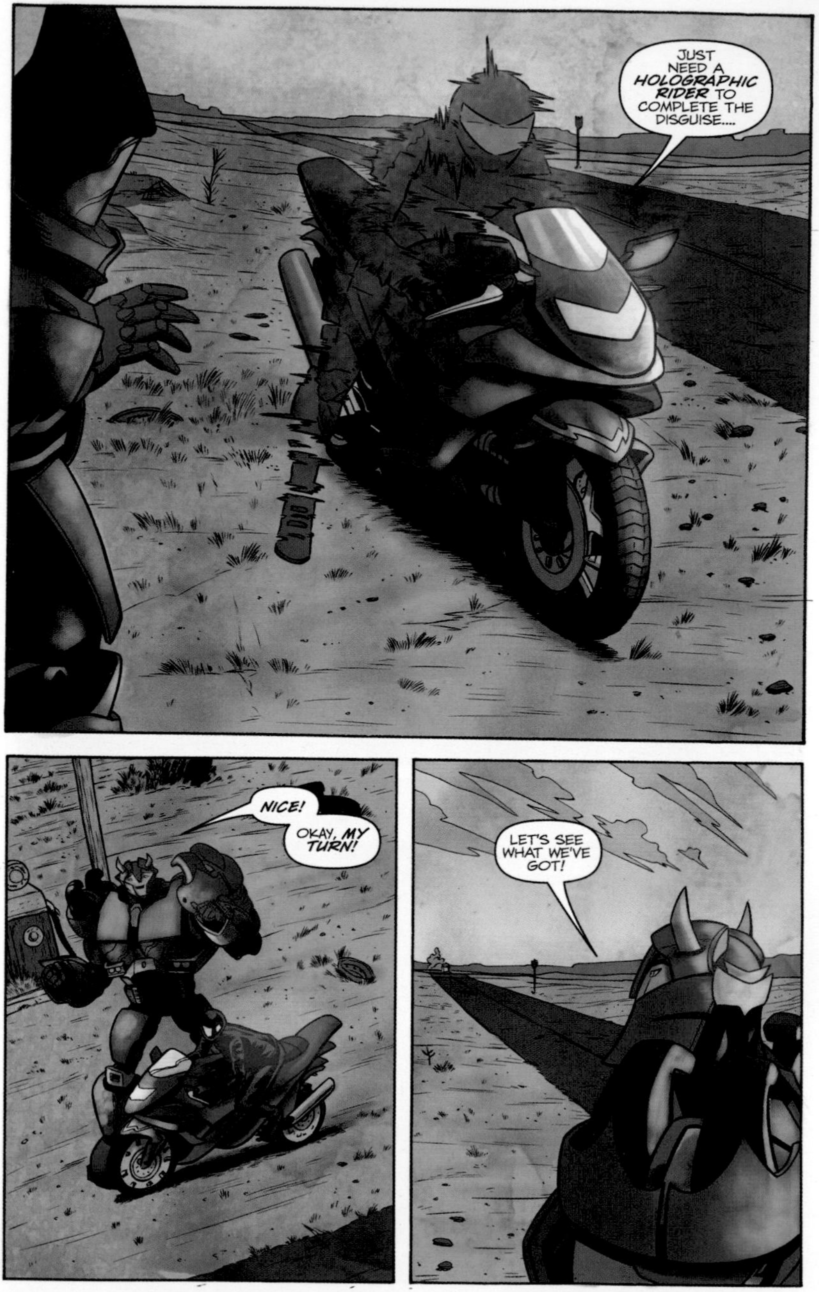
JUST NEED A HOLOGRAPHIC RIDER TO COMPLETE THE DISGUISE....
NICE!
OKAY, MY TURN!
LET'S SEE WHAT WE'VE GOT!

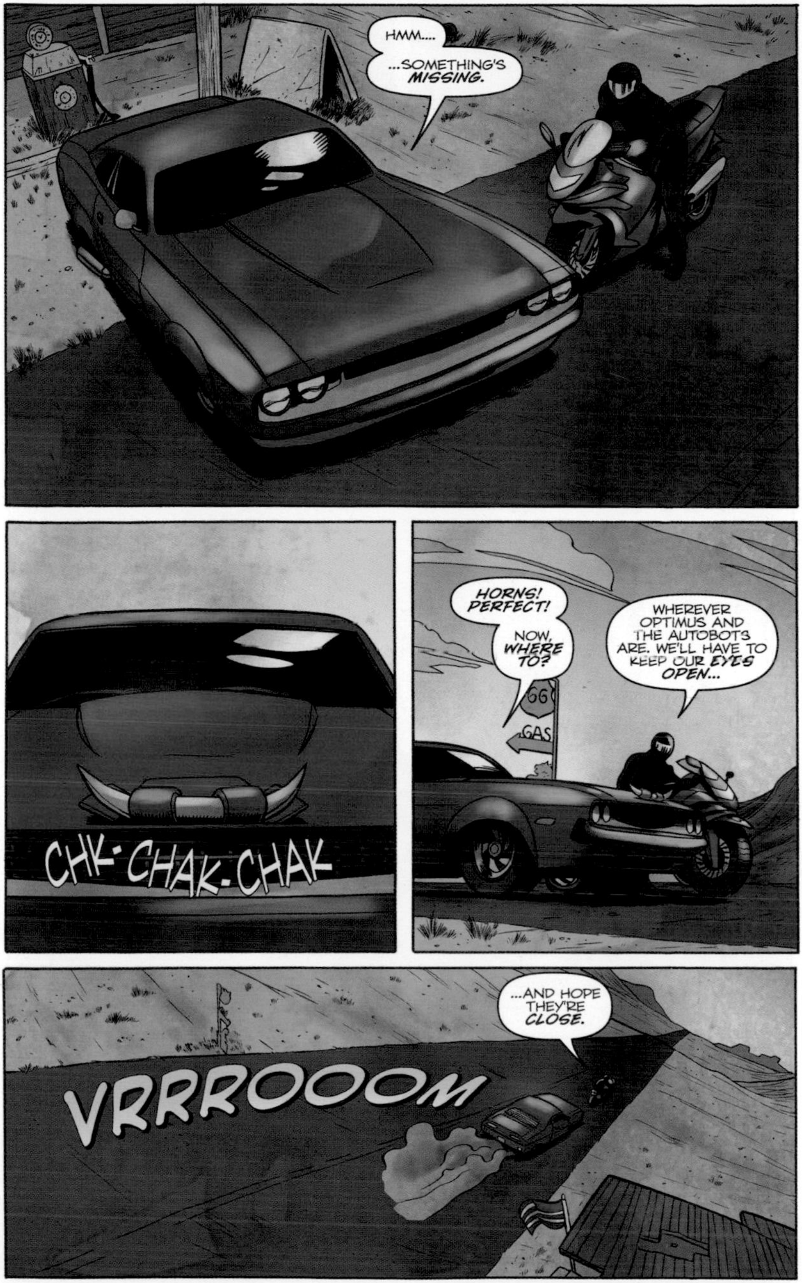
HMM....
...SOMETHING'S MISSING.
CHK-CHAK-CHAK
HORNS! PERFECT!
NOW, WHERE TO?
WHEREVER OPTIMUS AND THE AUTOBOTS ARE. WE'LL HAVE TO KEEP OUR EYES OPEN...
66
GAS
...AND HOPE THEY'RE CLOSE.
VRRROOOM

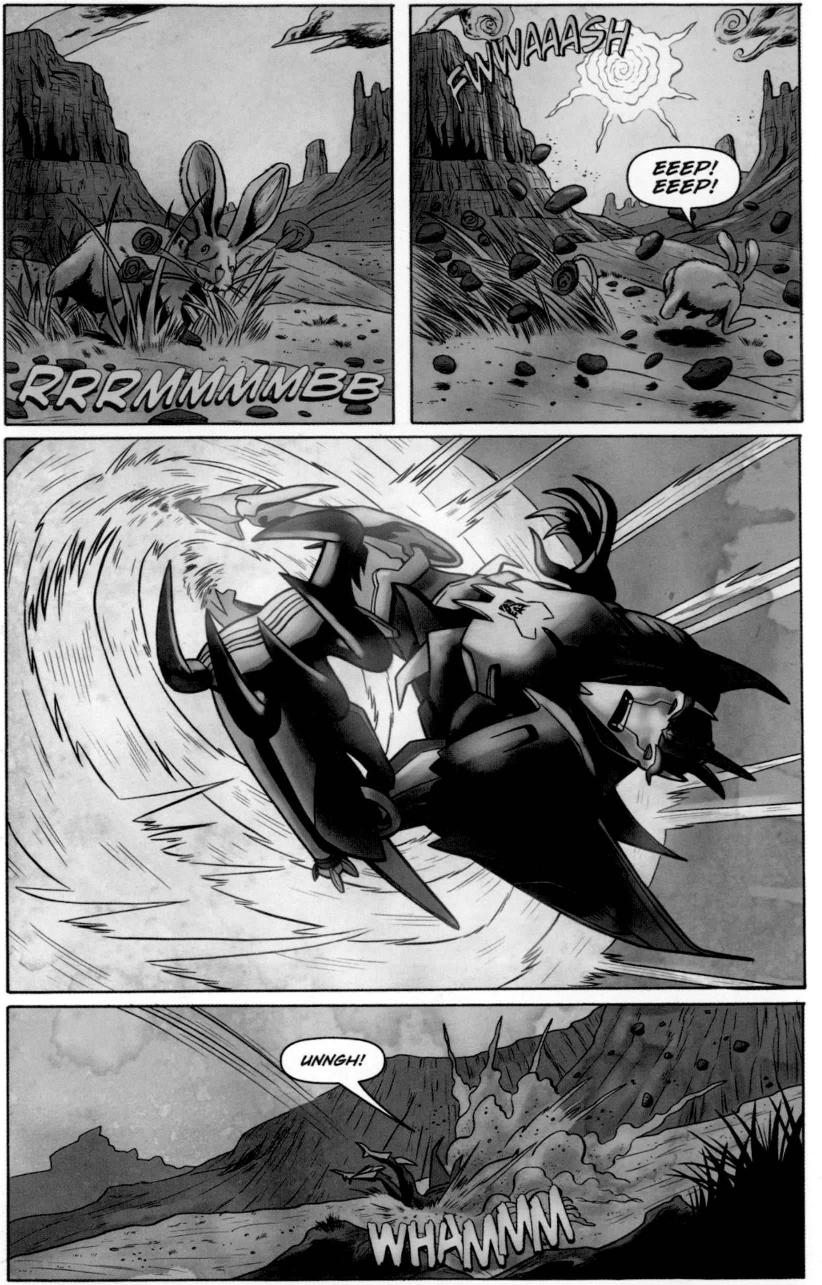
RRRMMMMMBB
FWWAAASH
EEEP! EEEP!
UNNGH!
WHAMMM

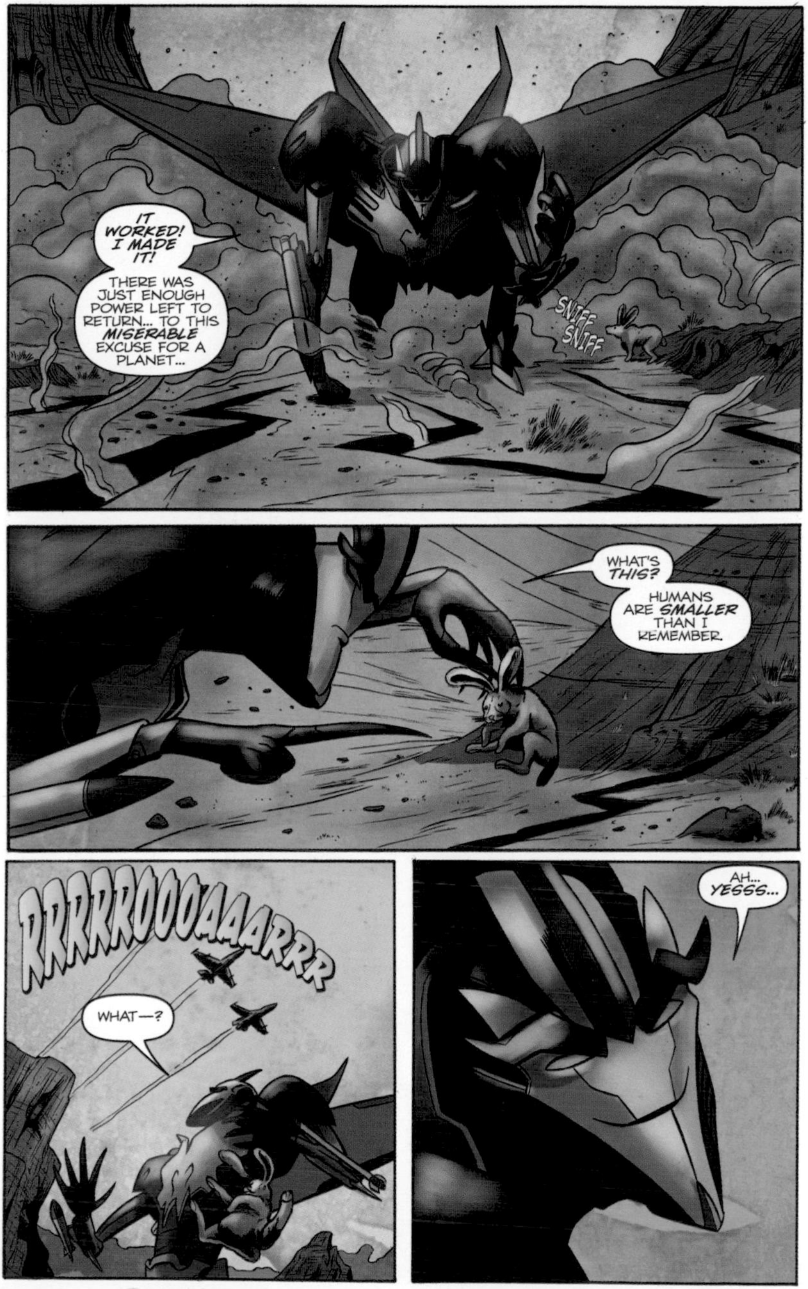
IT WORKED! I MADE IT!
THERE WAS JUST ENOUGH POWER LEFT TO RETURN... TO THIS MISERABLE EXCUSE FOR A PLANET...
SNIFF SNIFF
WHAT'S THIS?
HUMANS ARE SMALLER THAN I REMEMBER.
RRRRROOOAAAARRR
WHAT—?
AH... YESSS...

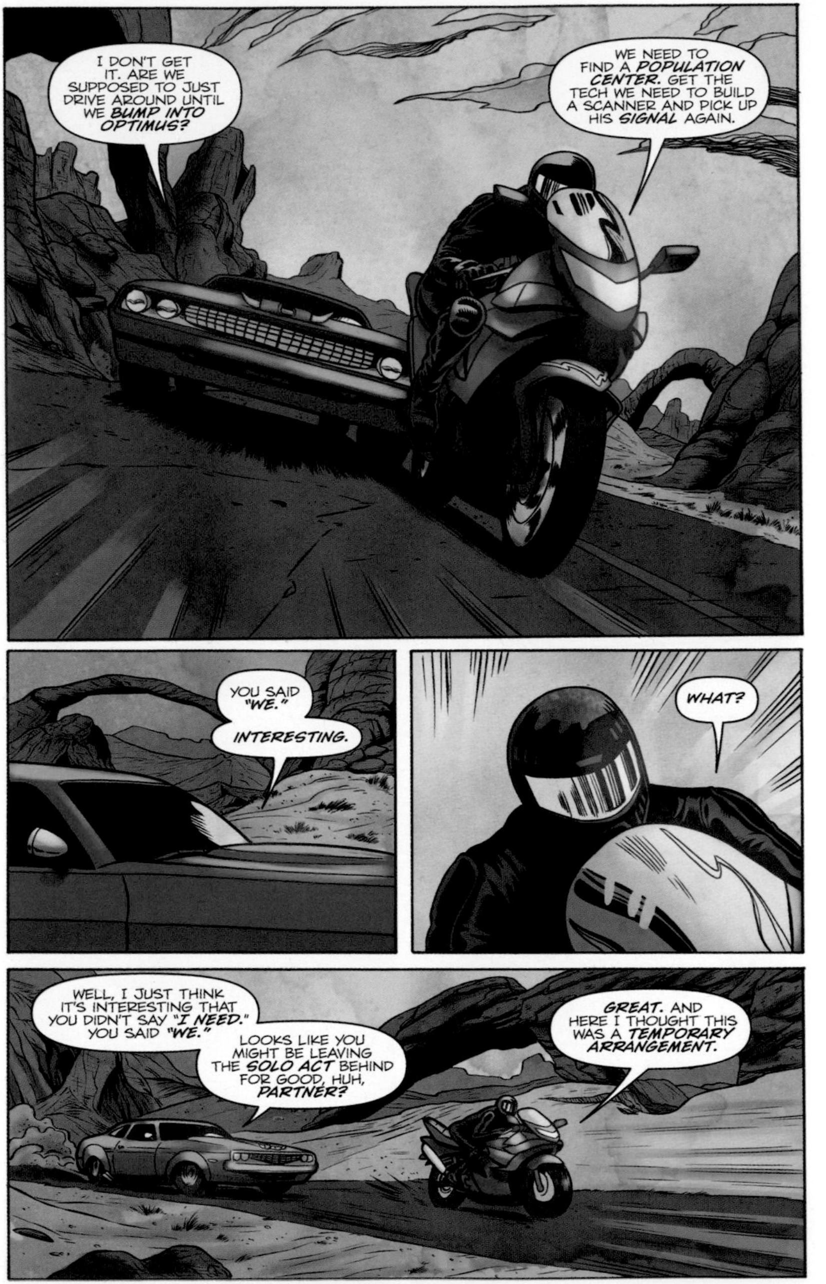

I DON'T GET IT. ARE WE SUPPOSED TO JUST DRIVE AROUND UNTIL WE BUMP INTO OPTIMUS?
WE NEED TO FIND A POPULATION CENTER. GET THE TECH WE NEED TO BUILD A SCANNER AND PICK UP HIS SIGNAL AGAIN.
YOU SAID "WE."
INTERESTING.
WHAT?
WELL, I JUST THINK IT'S INTERESTING THAT YOU DIDN'T SAY "I NEED." YOU SAID "WE."
LOOKS LIKE YOU MIGHT BE LEAVING THE SOLO ACT BEHIND FOR GOOD, HUH, PARTNER?
GREAT. AND HERE I THOUGHT THIS WAS A TEMPORARY ARRANGEMENT.

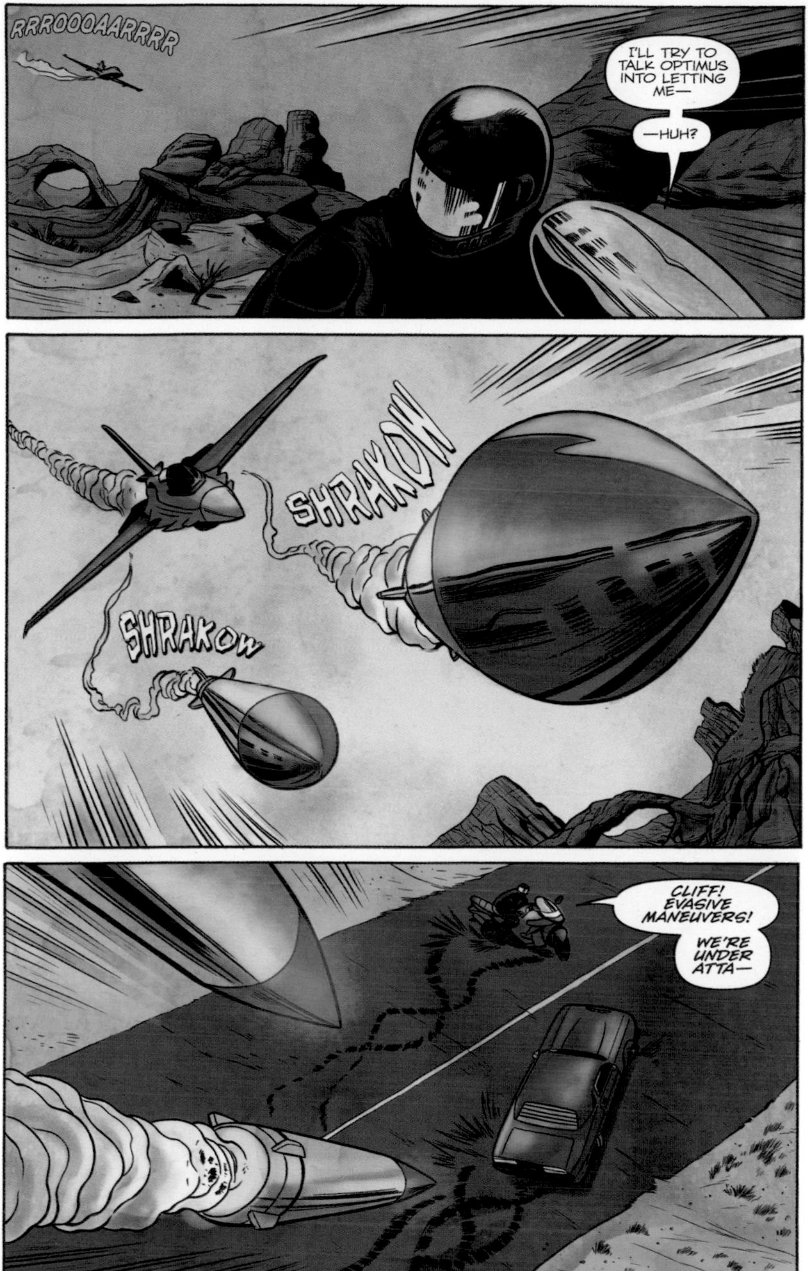
RRROOOAARRRR
I'LL TRY TO TALK OPTIMUS INTO LETTING ME—
—HUH?
SHRAKOW
SHRAKOW
CLIFF! EVASIVE MANEUVERS!
WE'RE UNDER ATTA—

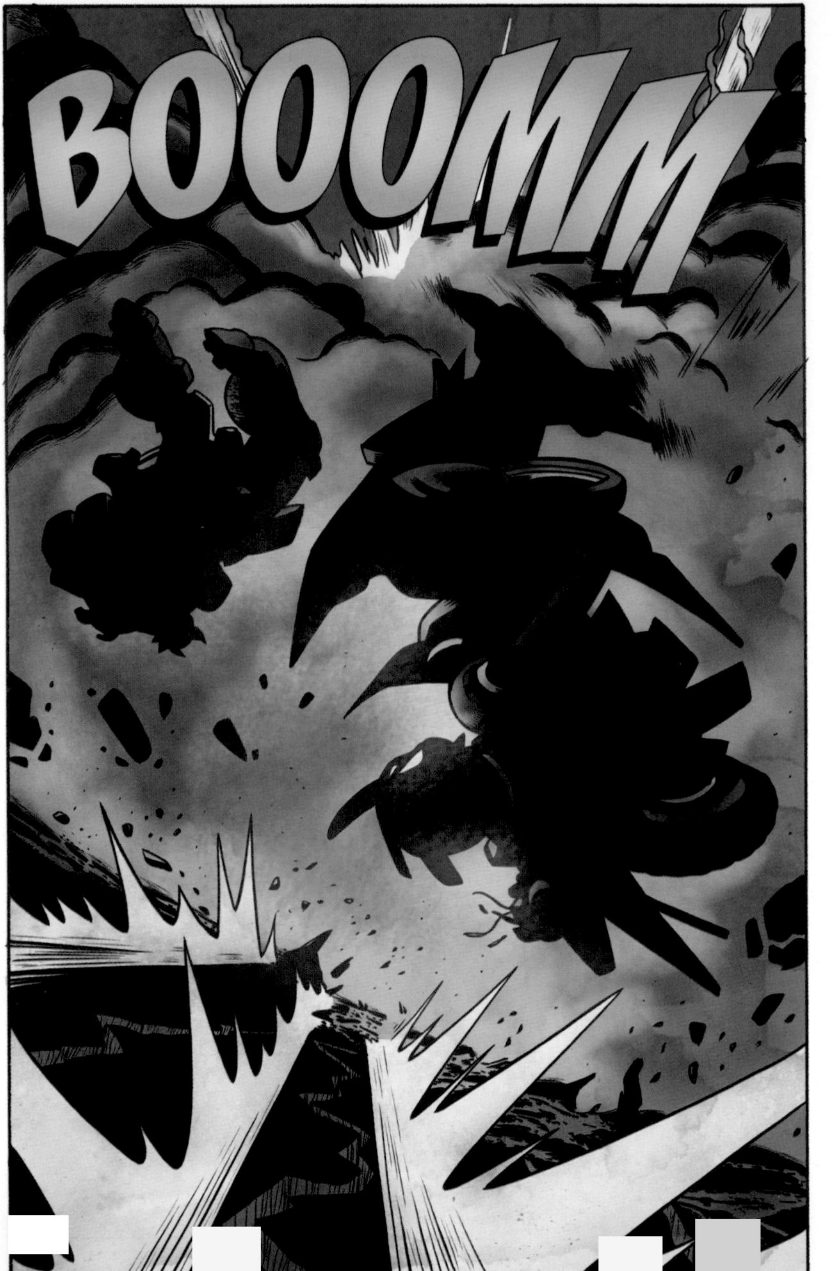
BOOOMM

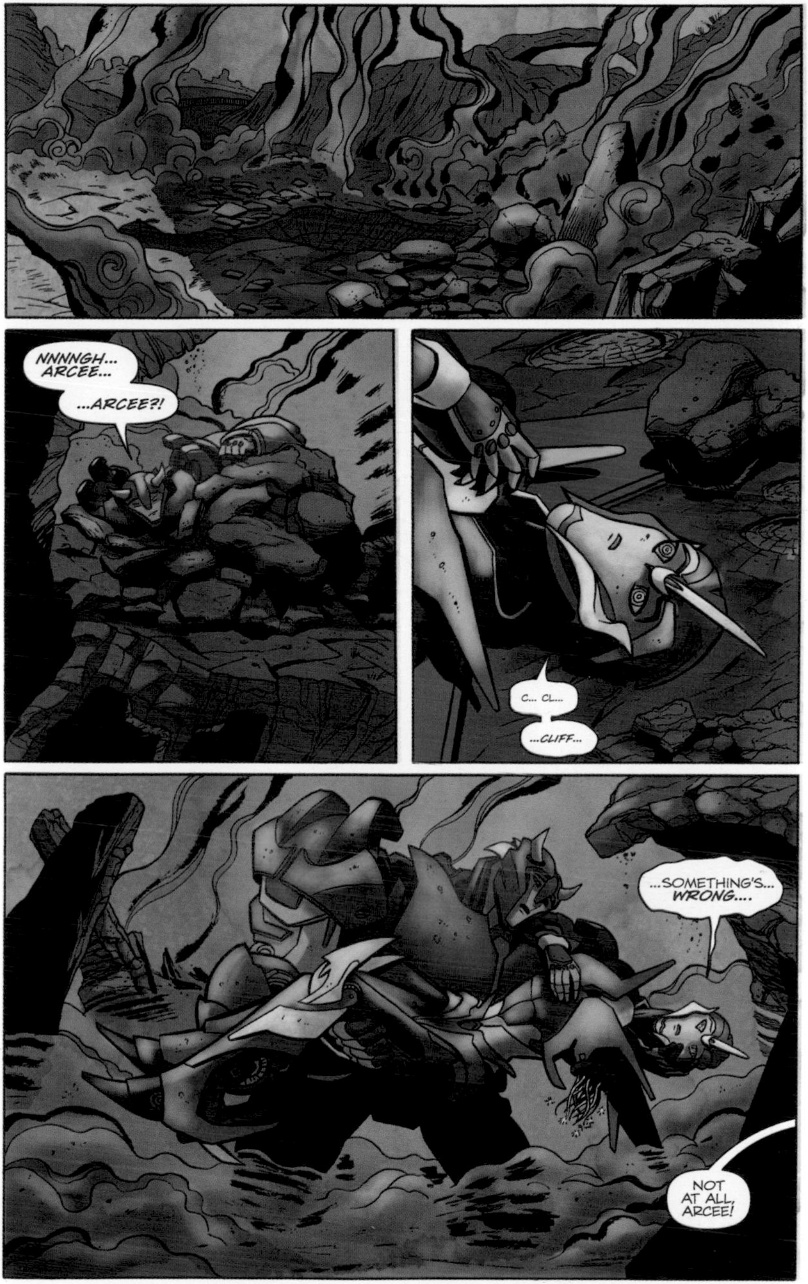

NNNNGH... ARCEE...
...ARCEE?!
C... CL...
...CLIFF...
...SOMETHING'S... WRONG....
NOT AT ALL, ARCEE!

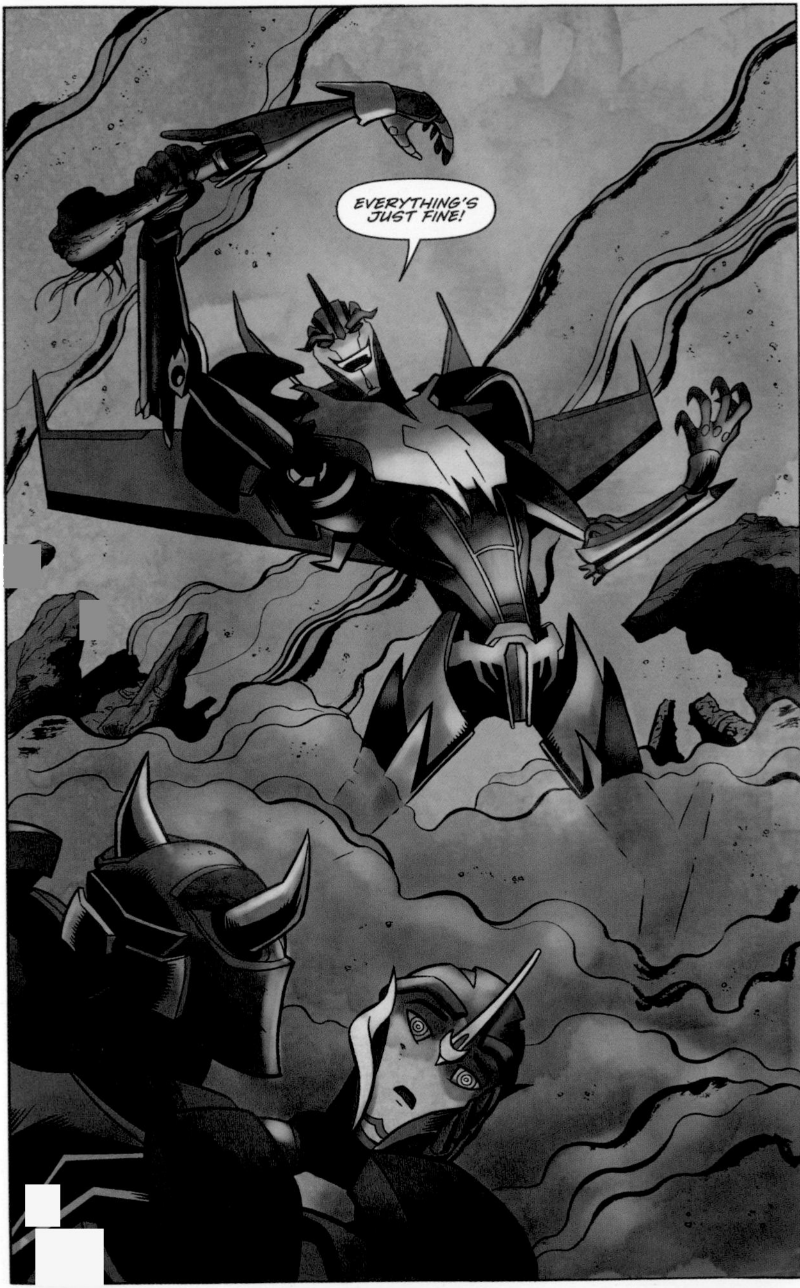
EVERYTHING'S JUST FINE!

Chapter Four

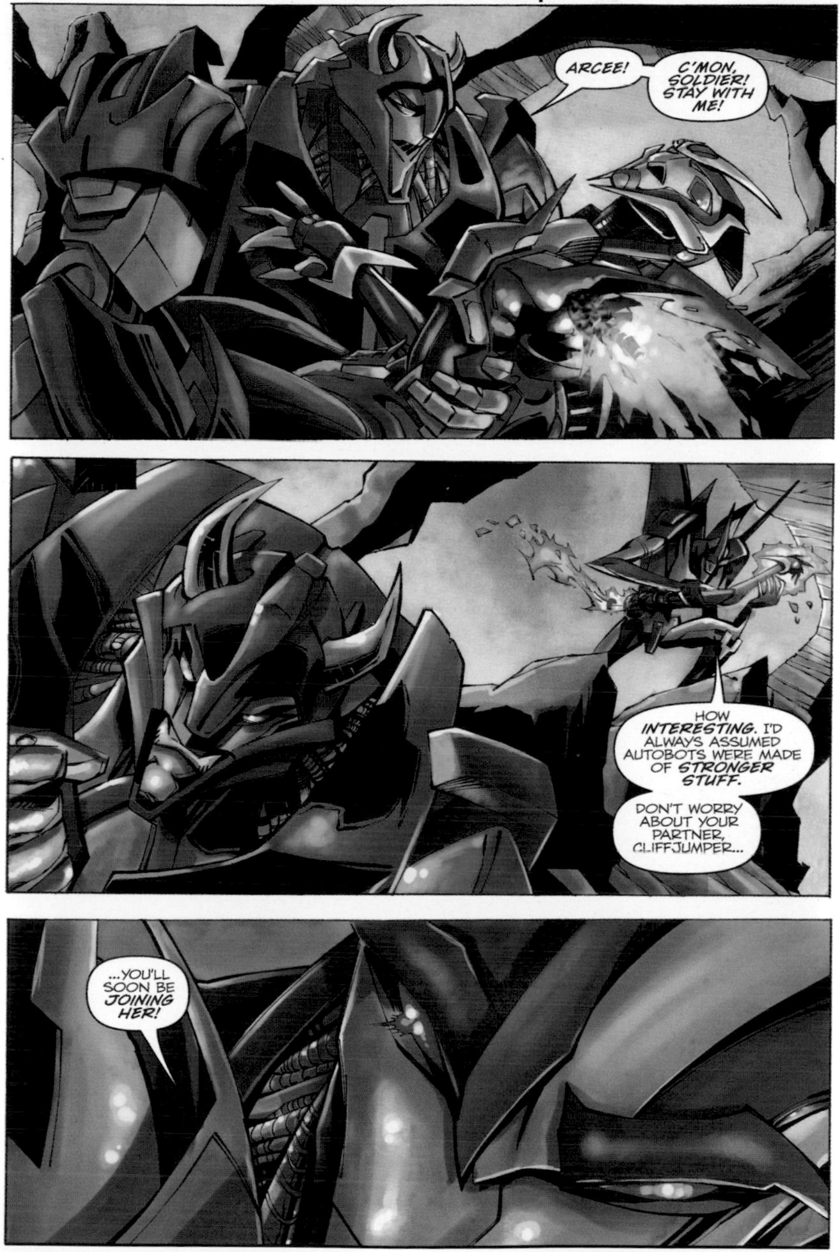
ARCEE!
C'MON, SOLDIER! STAY WITH ME!
HOW INTERESTING. I'D ALWAYS ASSUMED AUTOBOTS WERE MADE OF STRONGER STUFF.
DON'T WORRY ABOUT YOUR PARTNER, CLIFFJUMPER...
...YOU'LL SOON BE JOINING HER!

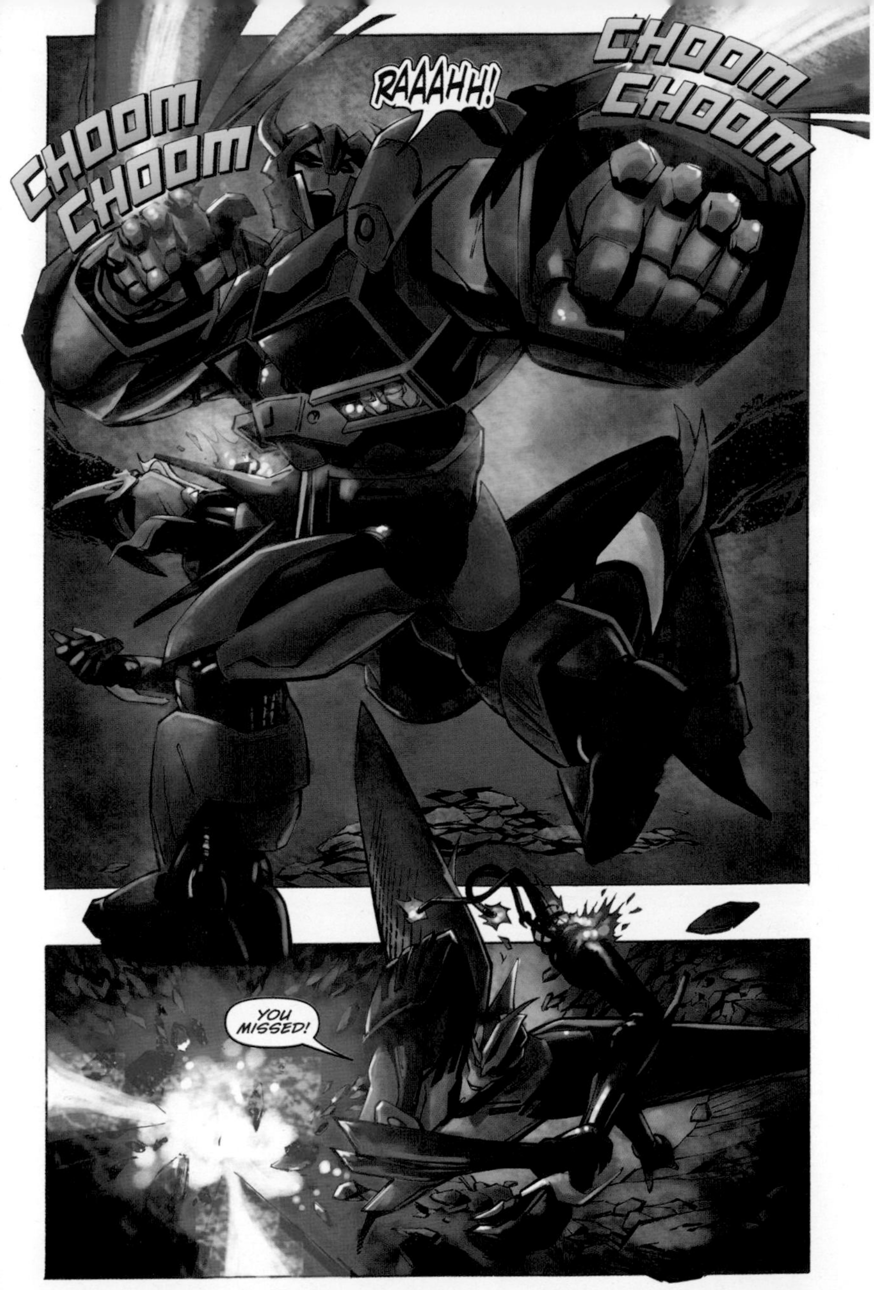
CHOOM CHOOM
RAAAHH!
CHOOM CHOOM
YOU MISSED!

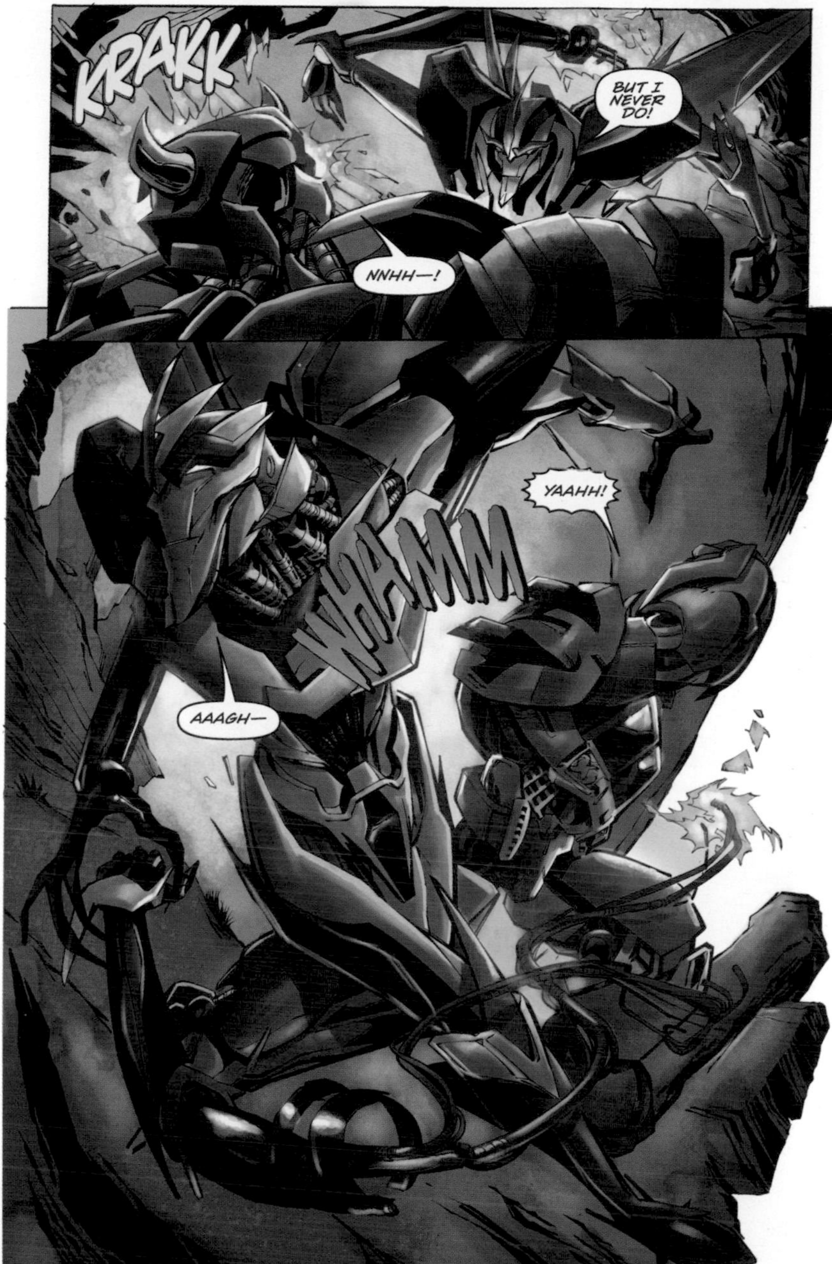
KRAKK
BUT I NEVER DO!
NNHH—!
YAAHH!
WHAMM
AAAGH—

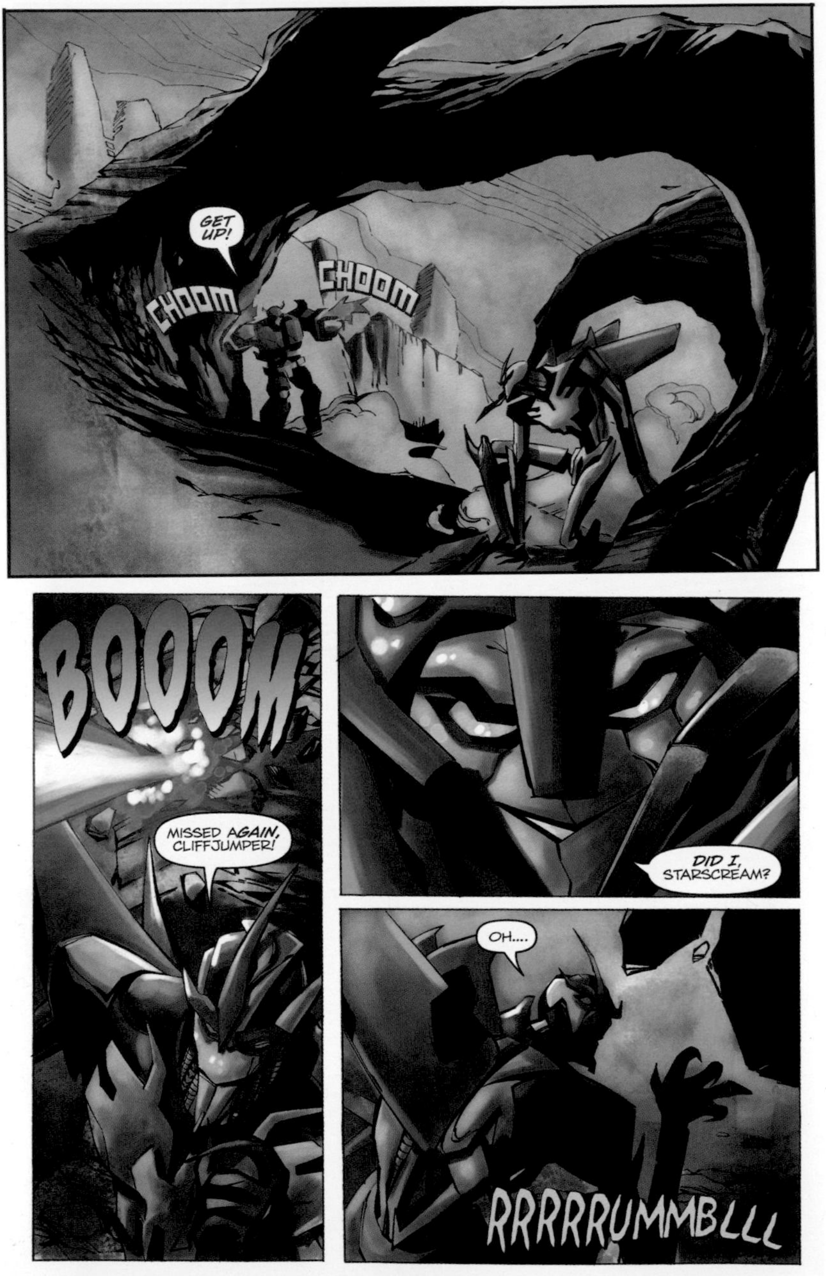
GET UP!
CHOOM
CHOOM
BOOOM
MISSED AGAIN, CLIFFJUMPER!
DID I, STARSCREAM?
OH....
RRRRRUMMBLLL

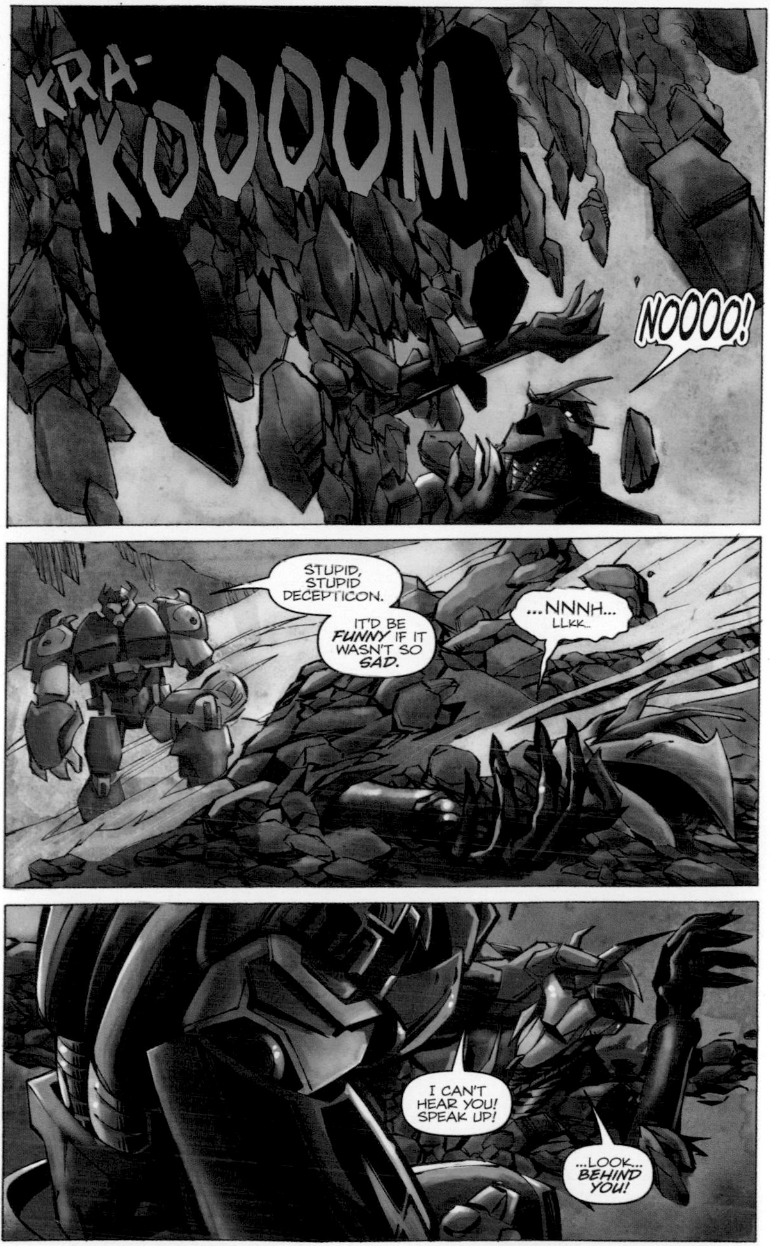
KRA-KOOOOOM
NOOOO!
STUPID, STUPID DECEPTICON.
IT'D BE FUNNY IF IT WASN'T SO SAD.
...NNNH... LLKK..
I CAN'T HEAR YOU! SPEAK UP!
...LOOK... BEHIND YOU!

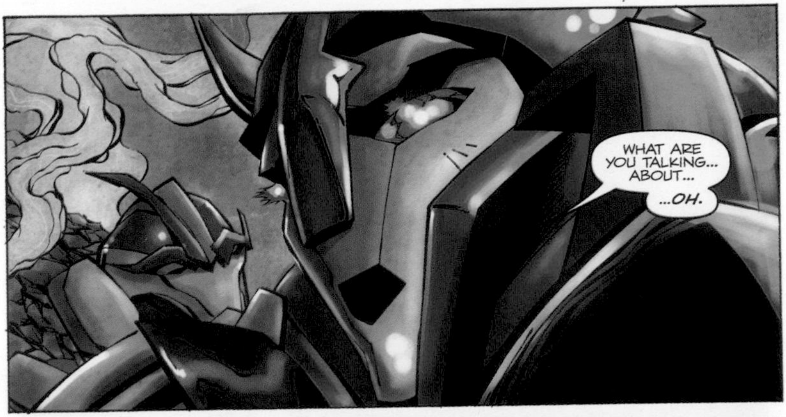
WHAT ARE YOU TALKING... ABOUT... ...OH.

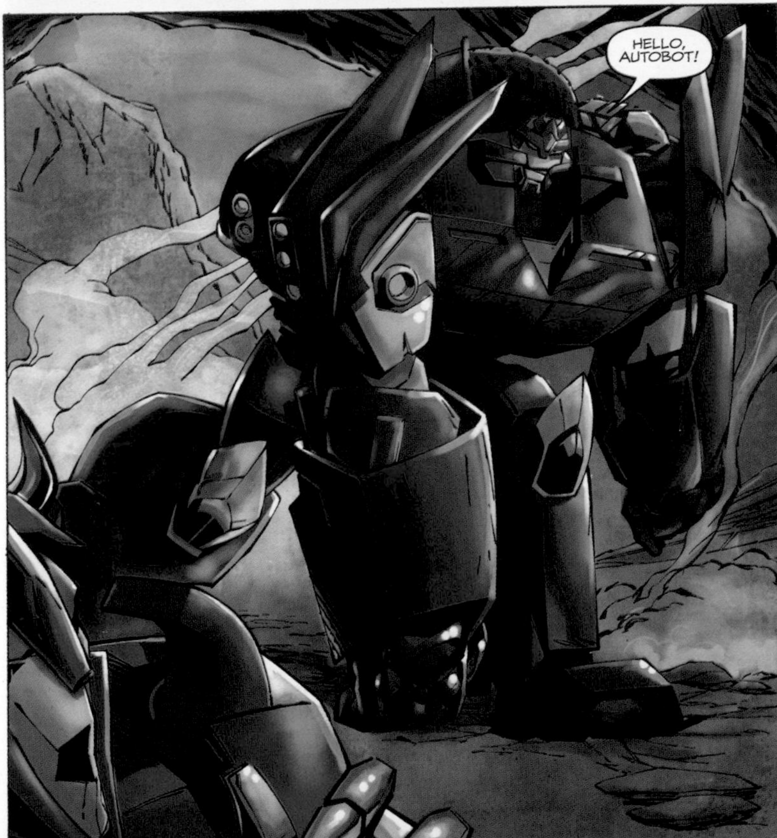
HELLO, AUTOBOT!

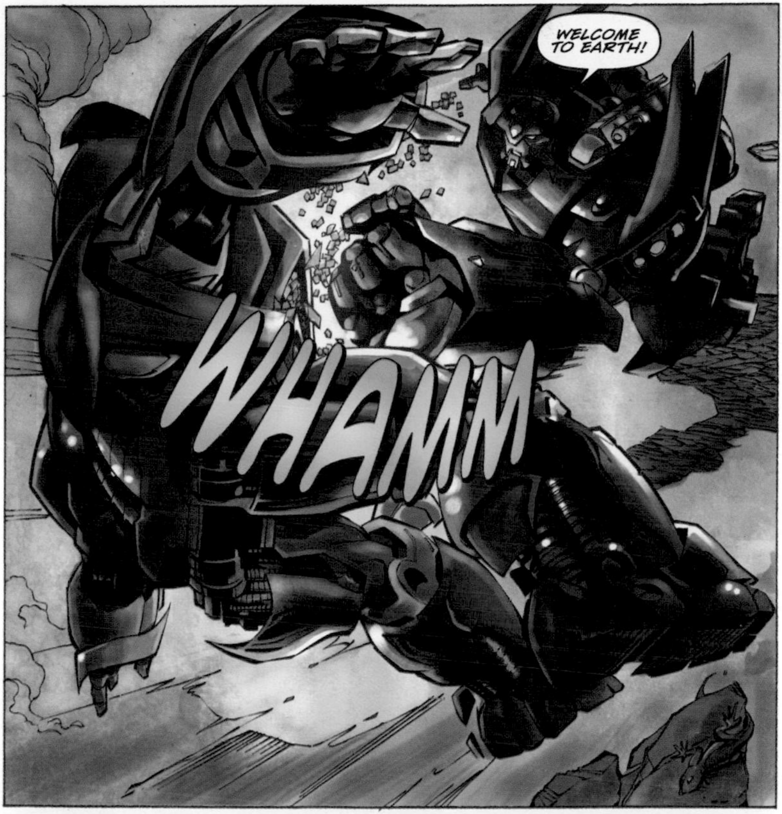
WELCOME TO EARTH!
WHAMM

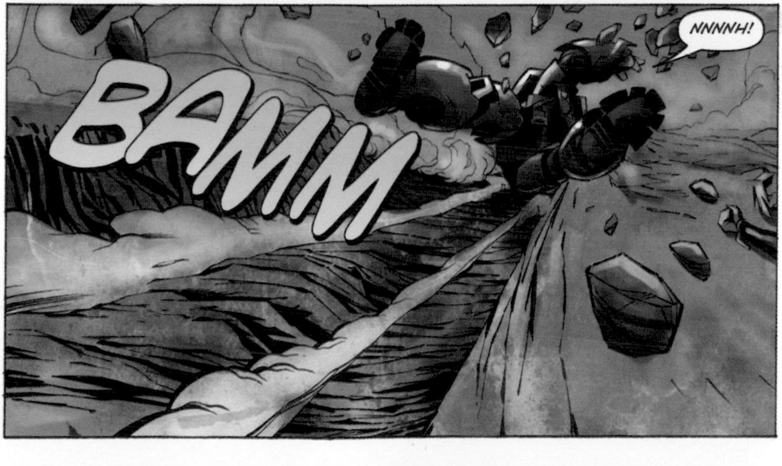
NNNNH!
BAMM

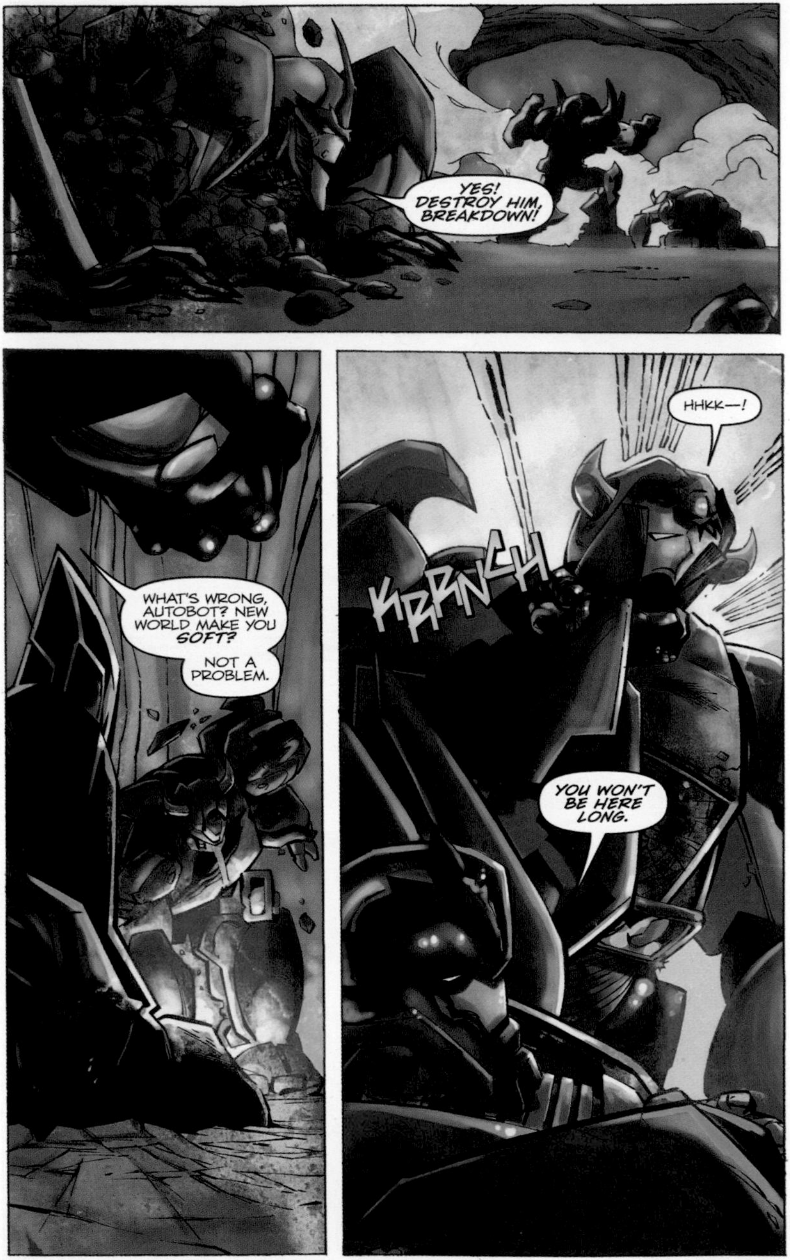
YES! DESTROY HIM, BREAKDOWN!
WHAT'S WRONG, AUTOBOT? NEW WORLD MAKE YOU SOFT?
NOT A PROBLEM.
HHKK—!
KRRNCH
YOU WON'T BE HERE LONG.

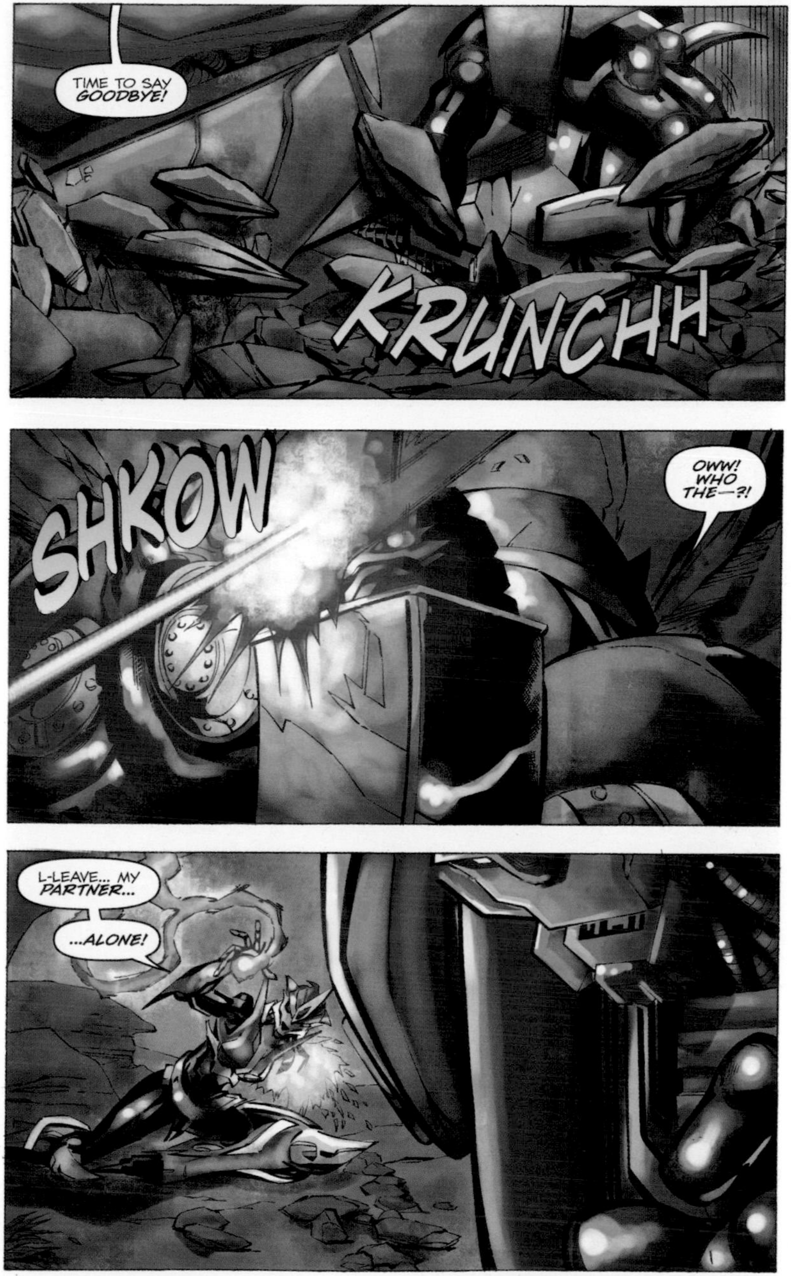
TIME TO SAY GOODBYE!
KRUNCHH
SHKOW
OWW! WHO THE—?!
L-LEAVE... MY PARTNER...
...ALONE!

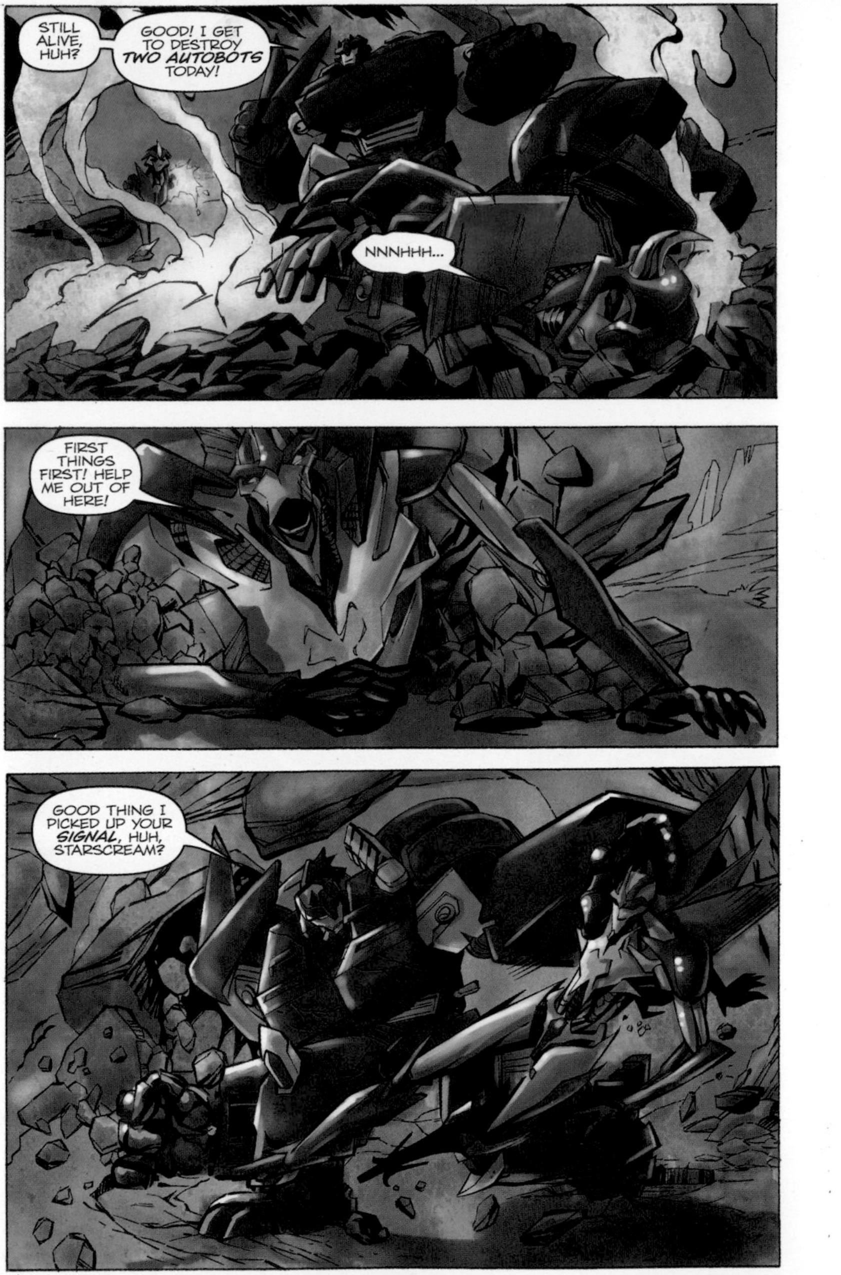
STILL ALIVE, HUH?
GOOD! I GET TO DESTROY TWO AUTOBOTS TODAY!
NNNHHH...
FIRST THINGS FIRST! HELP ME OUT OF HERE!
GOOD THING I PICKED UP YOUR SIGNAL, HUH, STARSCREAM?

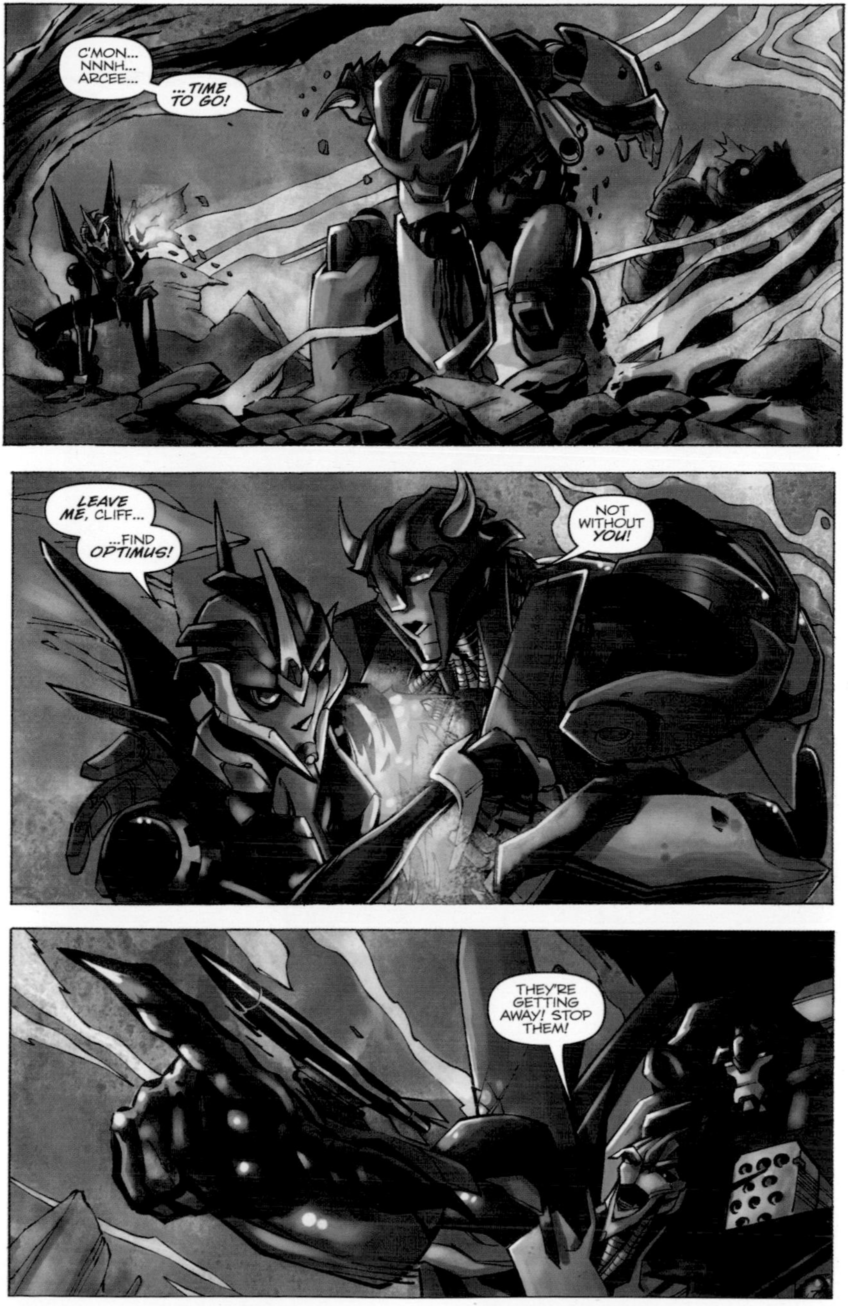

C'MON... NNNH... ARCEE...
...TIME TO GO!
LEAVE ME, CLIFF...
...FIND OPTIMUS!
NOT WITHOUT YOU!
THEY'RE GETTING AWAY! STOP THEM!

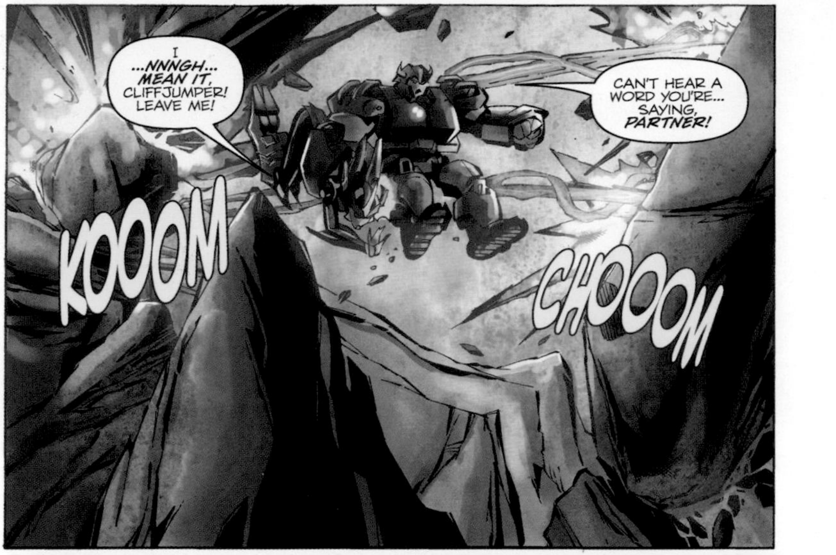
I ...NNNGH... MEAN IT, CLIFFJUMPER! LEAVE ME!
CAN'T HEAR A WORD YOU'RE... SAYING, PARTNER!
KOOOM
CHOOOM

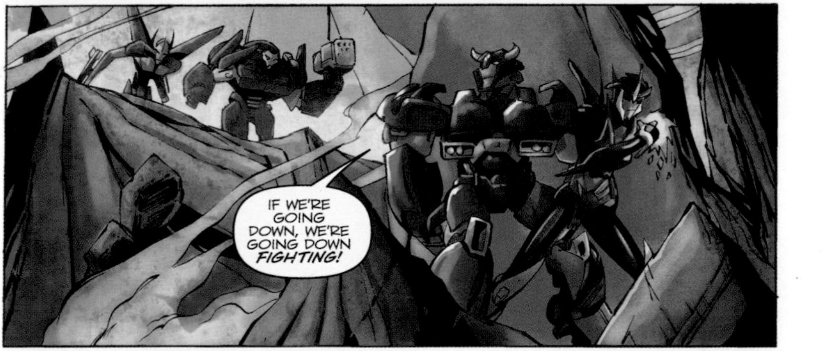
IF WE'RE GOING DOWN, WE'RE GOING DOWN FIGHTING!

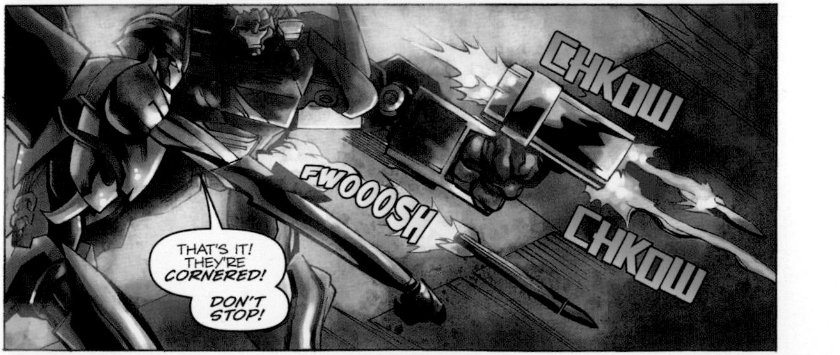
CHKOW
FWOOOSH
CHKOW
THAT'S IT! THEY'RE CORNERED!
DON'T STOP!

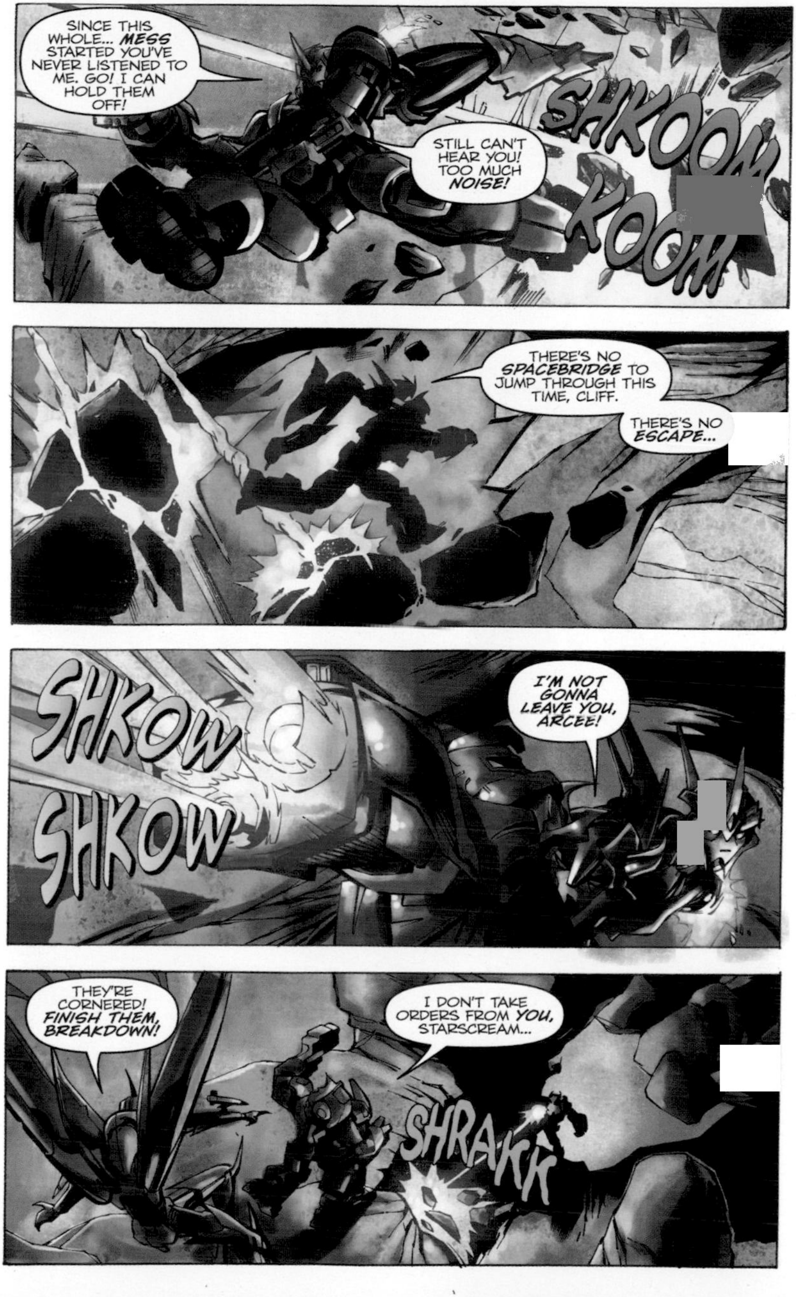
SINCE THIS WHOLE... MESS STARTED YOU'VE NEVER LISTENED TO ME. GO! I CAN HOLD THEM OFF!
STILL CAN'T HEAR YOU! TOO MUCH NOISE!
SHKOOM
KOOM
THERE'S NO SPACEBRIDGE TO JUMP THROUGH THIS TIME, CLIFF.
THERE'S NO ESCAPE...
SHKOW
SHKOW
I'M NOT GONNA LEAVE YOU, ARCEE!
THEY'RE CORNERED! FINISH THEM, BREAKDOWN!
I DON'T TAKE ORDERS FROM YOU, STARSCREAM...
SHRAKK

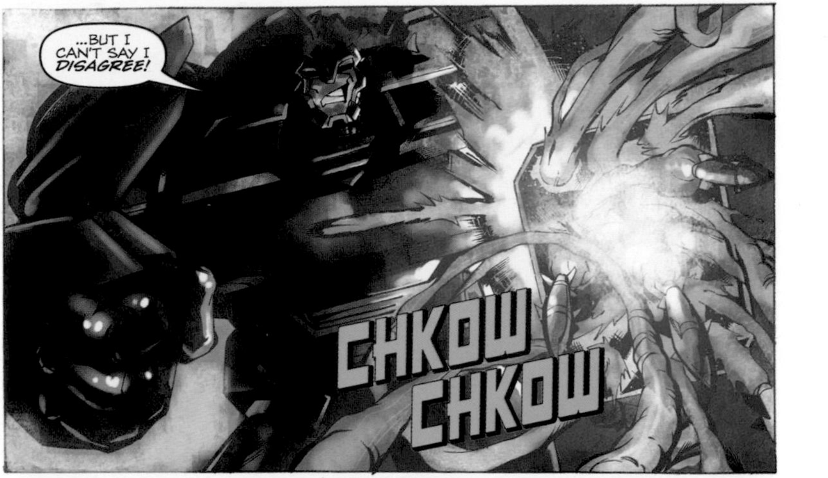
...BUT I CAN'T SAY I DISAGREE!
CHKOW CHKOW

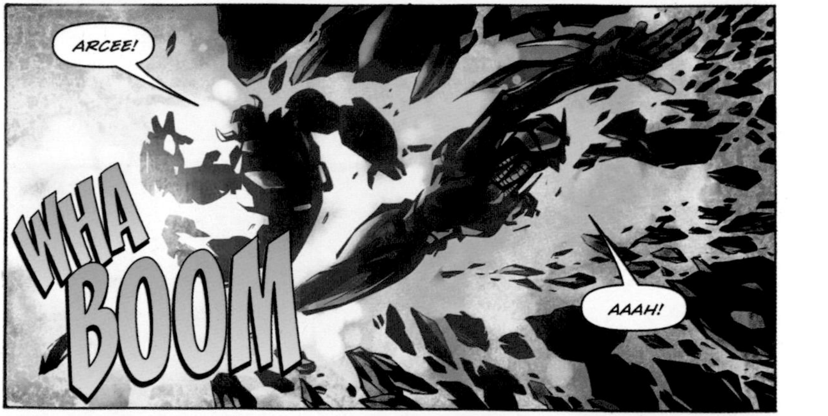
ARCEE!
WHA BOOM
AAAH!

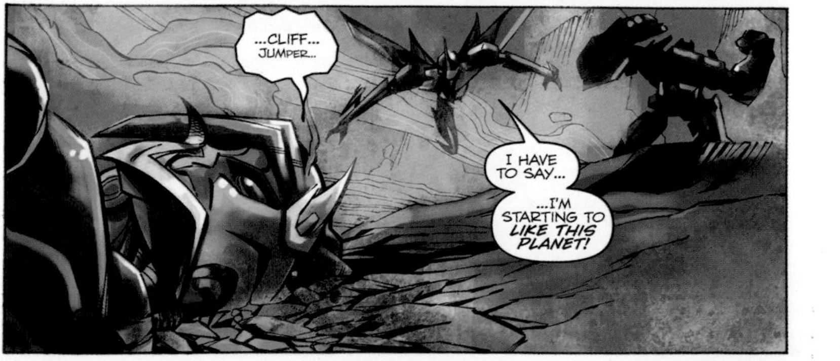
...CLIFF... JUMPER...
I HAVE TO SAY...
...I'M STARTING TO LIKE THIS PLANET!

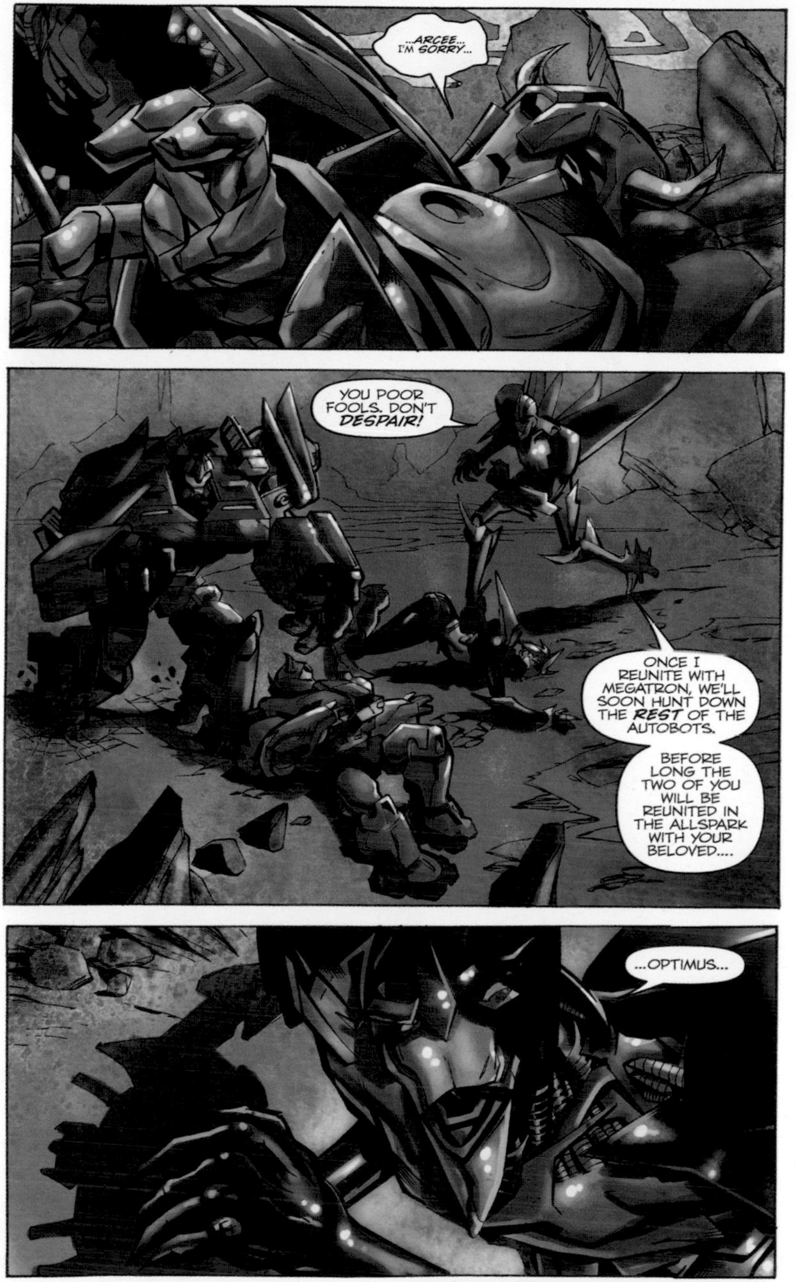
...ARCEE... I'M SORRY...
YOU POOR FOOLS. DON'T DESPAIR!
ONCE I REUNITE WITH MEGATRON, WE'LL SOON HUNT DOWN THE REST OF THE AUTOBOTS.
BEFORE LONG THE TWO OF YOU WILL BE REUNITED IN THE ALLSPARK WITH YOUR BELOVED....
...OPTIMUS...

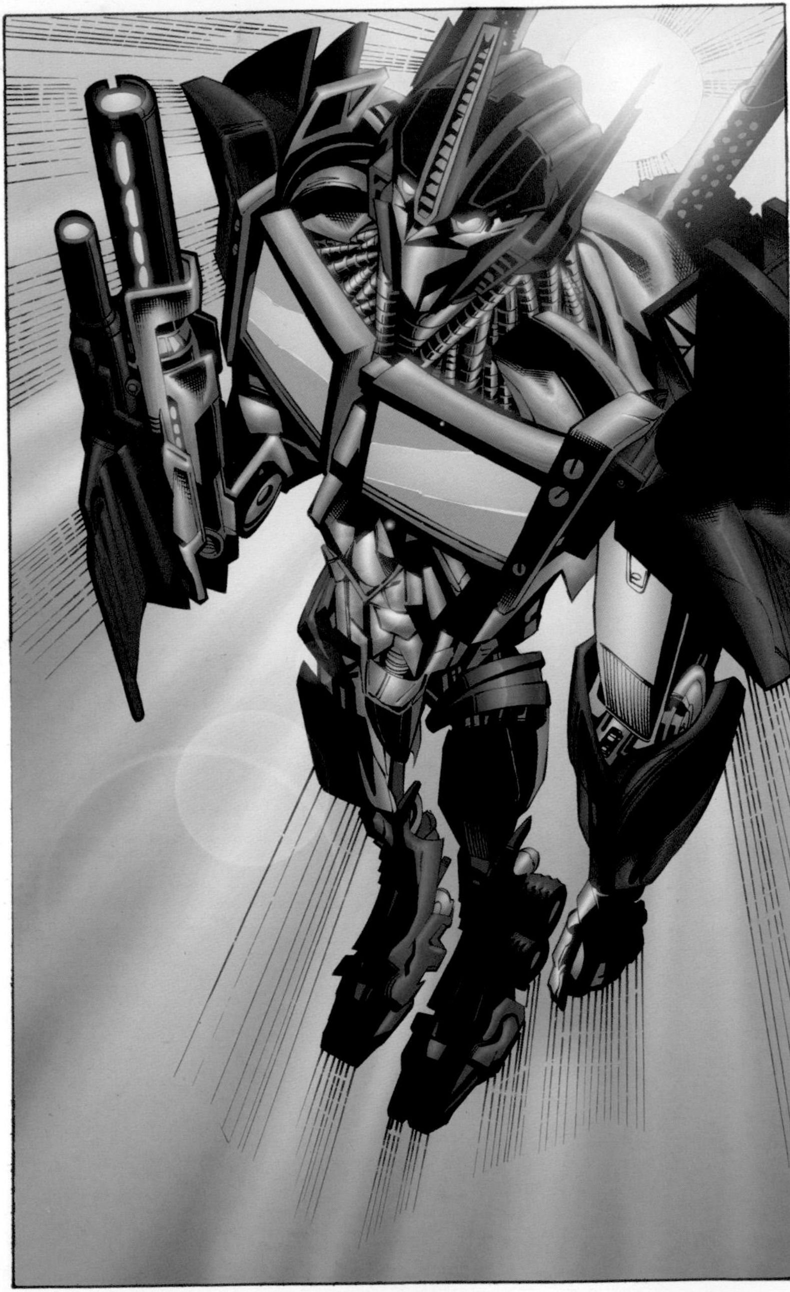

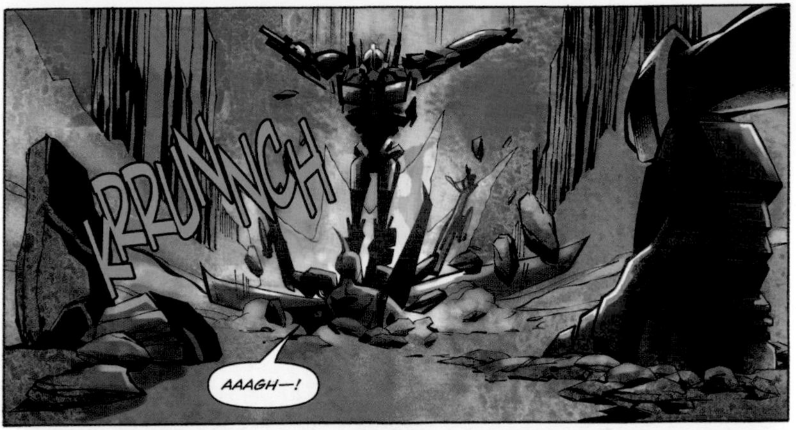
KRRUNNCH
AAAGH—!

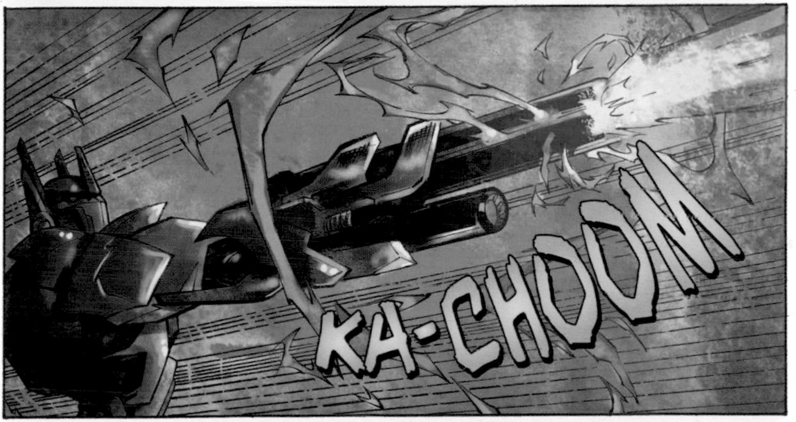
KA-CHOOM

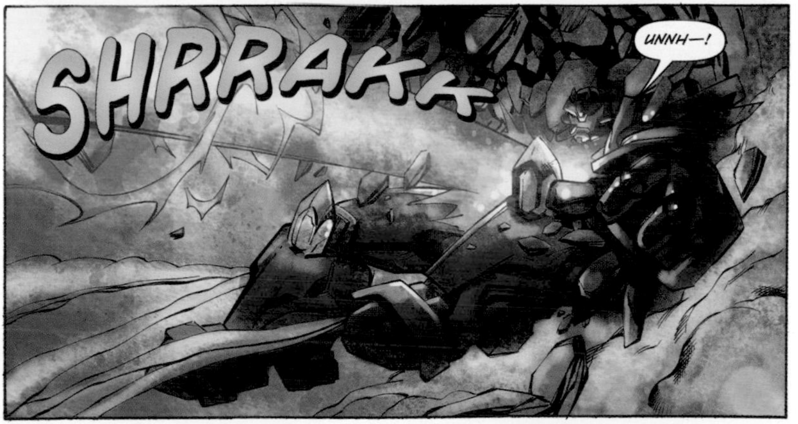
SHRRAKK
UNNH—!

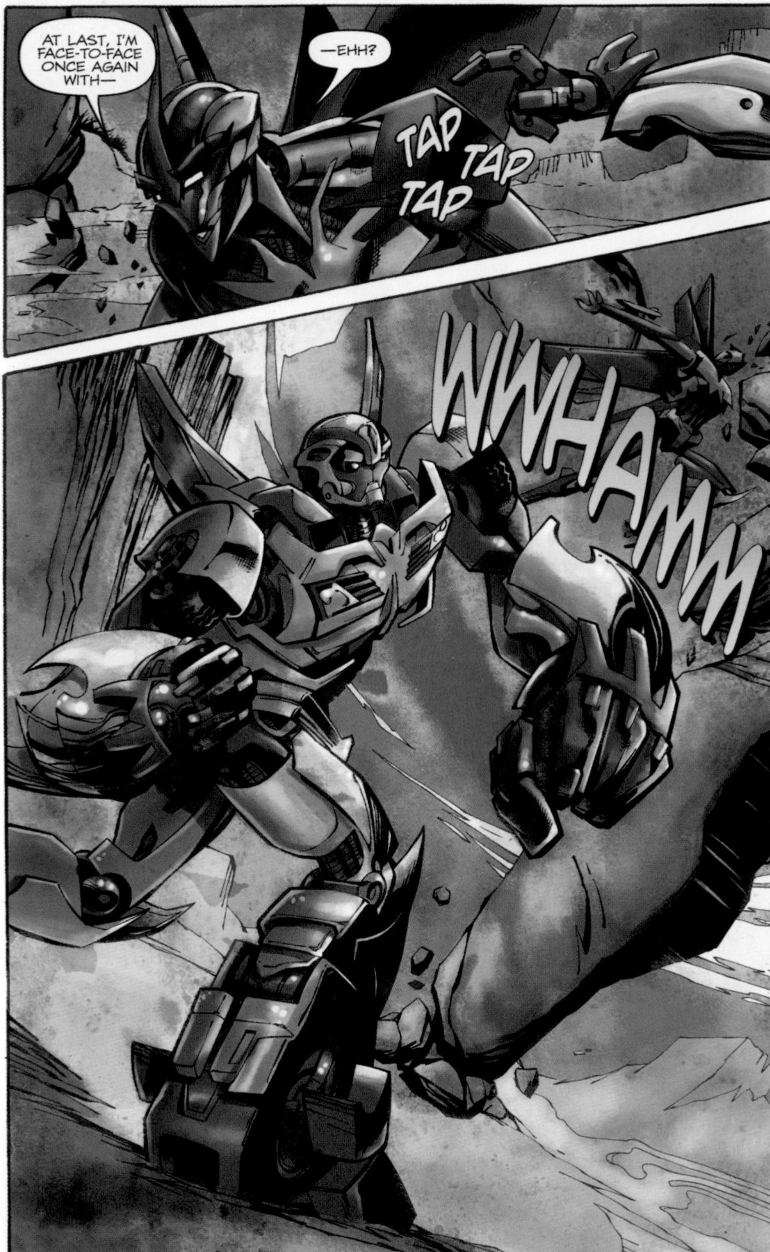
AT LAST, I'M FACE-TO-FACE ONCE AGAIN WITH—
—EHH?
TAP TAP TAP
WWHAMM

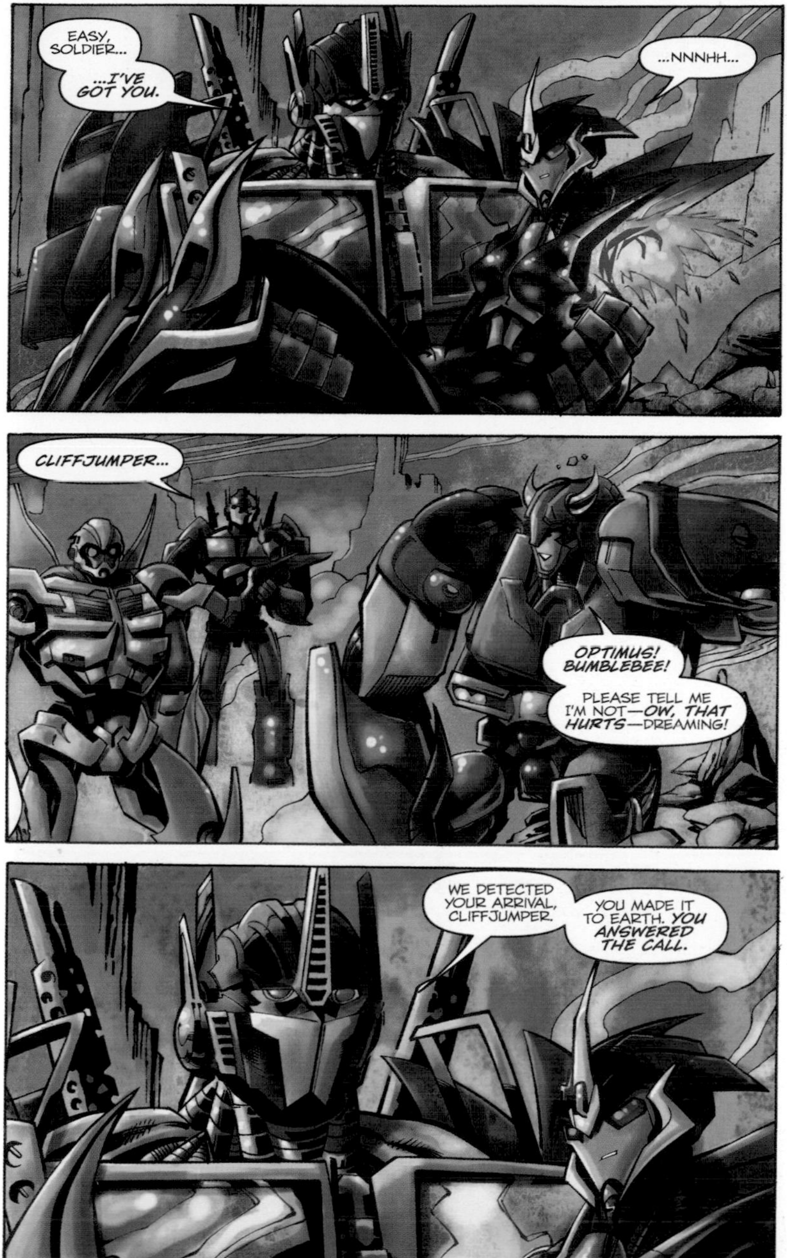
EASY, SOLDIER...
...I'VE GOT YOU.
...NNNHH...
CLIFFJUMPER...
OPTIMUS! BUMBLEBEE!
PLEASE TELL ME I'M NOT—OW, THAT HURTS—DREAMING!
WE DETECTED YOUR ARRIVAL, CLIFFJUMPER.
YOU MADE IT TO EARTH. YOU ANSWERED THE CALL.

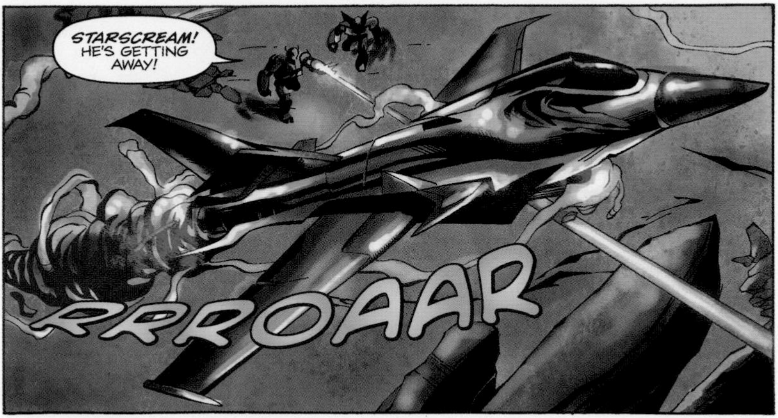
STARSCREAM! HE'S GETTING AWAY!
RRROAAR

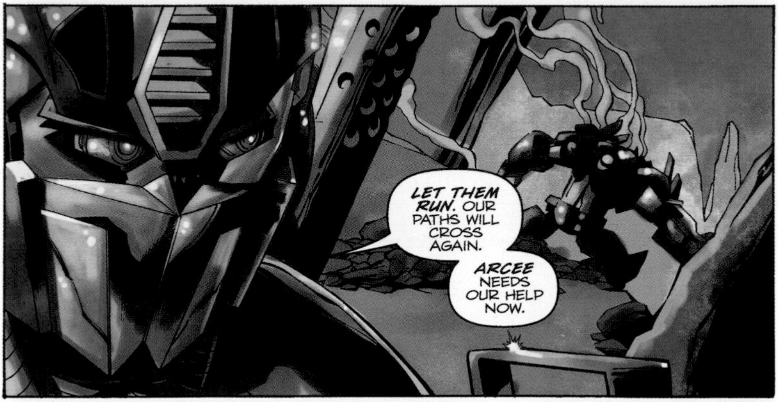
LET THEM RUN. OUR PATHS WILL CROSS AGAIN.
ARCEE NEEDS OUR HELP NOW.

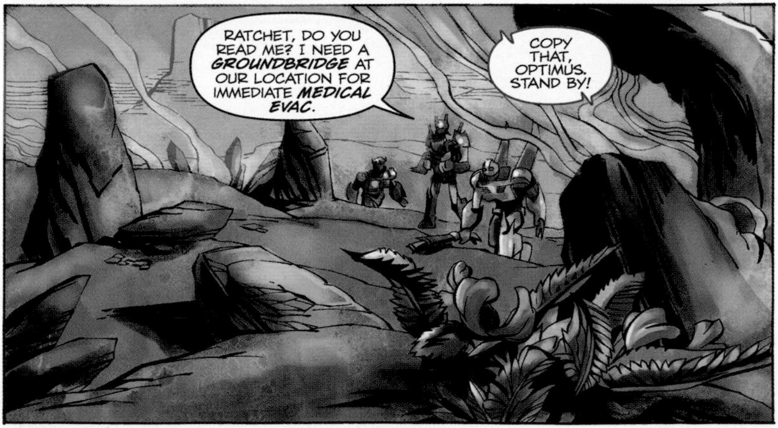
RATCHET, DO YOU READ ME? I NEED A GROUNDBRIDGE AT OUR LOCATION FOR IMMEDIATE MEDICAL EVAC.
COPY THAT, OPTIMUS. STAND BY!

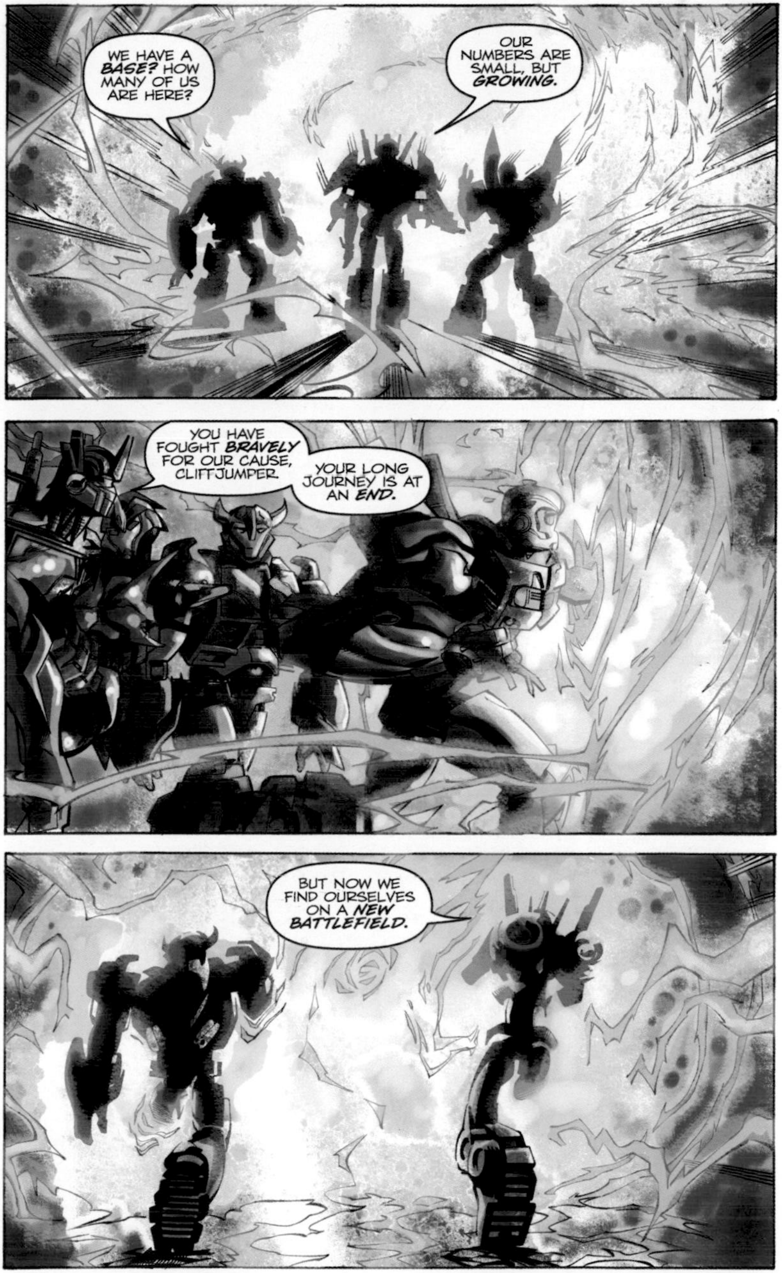
WE HAVE A *BASE?* HOW MANY OF US ARE HERE?
OUR NUMBERS ARE SMALL, BUT *GROWING.*
YOU HAVE FOUGHT *BRAVELY* FOR OUR CAUSE, CLIFFJUMPER.
YOUR LONG JOURNEY IS AT AN *END.*
BUT NOW WE FIND OURSELVES ON A *NEW BATTLEFIELD.*

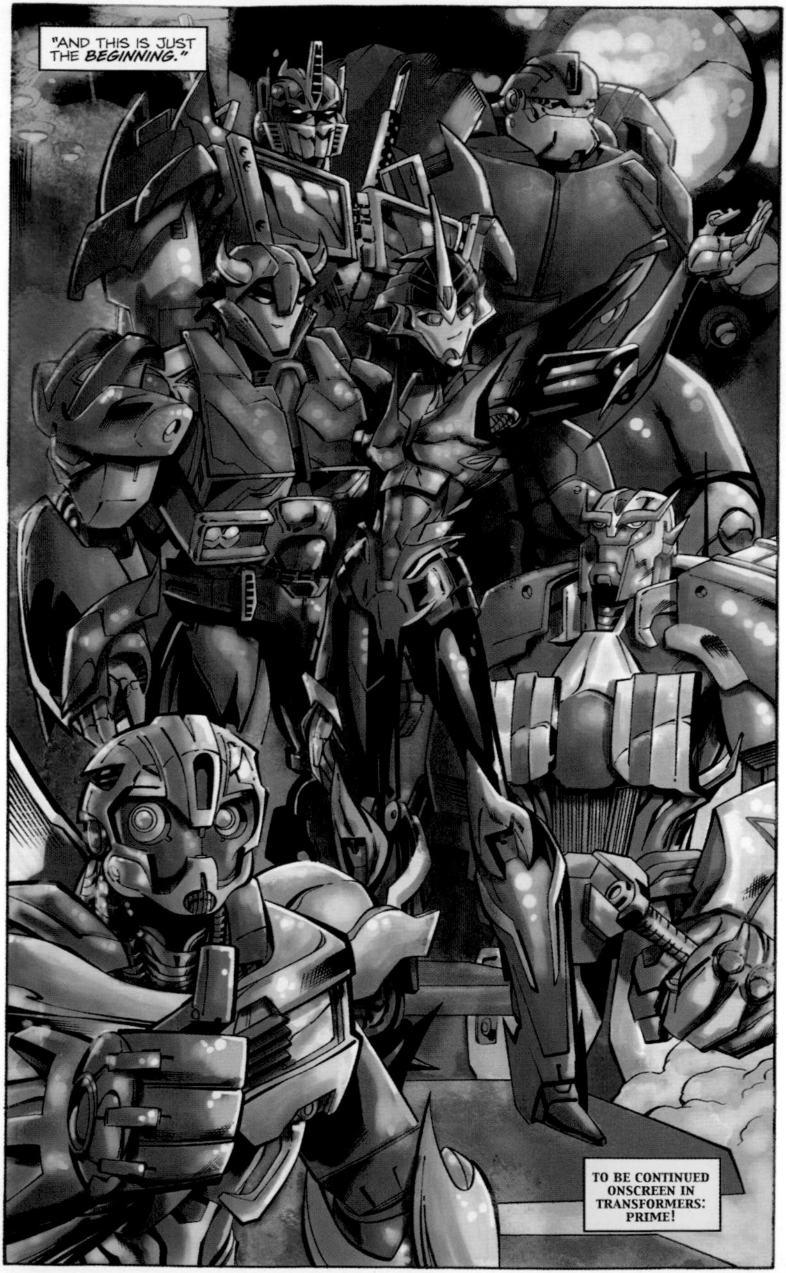
"AND THIS IS JUST THE *BEGINNING.*"
TO BE CONTINUED ONSCREEN IN TRANSFORMERS: PRIME!